On the Lamb

in a
Doggy Dog World

At Play with the English Language

ALSO BY MICHAEL SHEEHAN

The Word Parts Dictionary

Words!~ A Vocabulary Power Workbook

Handbook for Basic Writers

Workbook for Basic Writers

The Cry of the Jackal

In the Shadow of the Bear

Words to the Wise: A Lighthearted Look at the English Language

On the Lamb
in a
Doggy Dog World

At Play with the English Language

Michael J. Sheehan

MICHAEL J. SHEEHAN

A

ARBUTUS PRESS
TRAVERSE CITY, MICHIGAN

On the Lamb in a Doggy Dog World: At Play with the English Language

ISBN-13: 978-0-9766104-9-6
ISBN-10: 0-9766104-9-3

Arbutus Press
Traverse City, Michigan
www.Arbutuspress.com

Library of Congress Cataloging-in-Publication Data

Sheehan, Michael, 1939-
   On the lamb in a doggy dog world : at play with the English language / Michael J. Sheehan.
      p. cm.
   ISBN-13: 978-0-9766104-9-6
   ISBN-10: 0-9766104-9-3
   1. Lexicology. 2. English language—Etymology. 3. Figures of speech. 4. Vocabulary. 5. Play on words. 6. English language—Humor. I. Title.

   PE1574.S54 2006
   423'.028—dc22
                                        2006013204

Printed in the United States of America

DEDICATION

To my brother Frank,
an unleashed survivor in a dog-eat-dog world.

CONTENTS

PREFACE

A few seasons back, a local work-release prisoner failed to turn up one night at the appointed time to occupy his jail bunk. When he was caught after barely a week of freedom, headline writers in two papers praised the long arm of the law: Prisoner captured on the lamb. My immediate reaction was that he must have felt quite sheepish. He hadn't been able to pull the wool over their eyes.

Errors such as this lurk on every side. We see "Muscle Salad" in a delicatessen. The crawling headlines at the bottom of the TV screen reveal that "Republicans are diabolically opposed to new tax hike." A radio announcer instructs us that flags are to be lowered to "half mass" to honor those recently killed in battle.

In most cases, people are writing what they have heard—or thought they heard—rather than reproducing a phrase that they saw in print. It's reminiscent of the old parlor game, Telephone. In that game from the era of innocence, players would sit in a circle. The first person would lean over and whisper a phrase in the next person's ear, perhaps something like big blue baby buggy bumpers. The second person would whisper what she heard into the next person's ear, and so on down the line. When it came back to the first person, he was often reduced to gales of laughter at the massive distortion that had taken place. When he shared the original and the final versions with the other players, it was always good for a laugh. Simpler times.

This book has fun with language. Among other things, it considers student bloopers, names that are eerily appropriate to the profession of the bearer, puns, Irish Bulls (self-contradictory statements), wacky combinations based on firm names and movie titles, malaprops and mondegreens, and the unintentional humor found in dangling modifiers.

Because language runs the entire gamut of emotions and reactions, this book has a serious side, too. We will observe how dictionaries handle the definitions of colors, an inescapably visual—not verbal—experience. We will also consider phrases with a nautical origin, specialized names for experts, popular language myths circulating as truth on the internet, and some interesting word histories. Finally there will be a list of a few language web sites that can be trusted; there's a lot of garbage floating out there.

The chapters may be read in random fashion, depending on your mood of the day. There is no central thesis at work here, just an appreciation and awe of language itself. I should mention that many of these essays originally appeared in some form on *The Vocabula Review,* an online language e-zine found at http://www.vocabula.com/

Michael J. Sheehan
May 2006
wordmall@aol.com

STUDENT BLOOPERS

A blooper is defined as an embarrassing public blunder, but as long as it's someone else's mistake, most of us are quite capable of getting past the embarrassment to enjoy the humor. Not only have books appeared in recent years to document and preserve bloopers, but TV shows on the subject have delighted in exposing human fallibility, too—especially when authority figures are involved.

The word *blooper*, which first showed up between 1925 and 1930, has an interesting origin. In the early days of radio, a receiving set that wasn't finely tuned could generate antenna frequency signals that interfered with other nearby receivers. Based on what someone in those days thought they sounded like, these high-pitched sounds came to be called bloops, and the offending receiver was called a blooper.

The following bloopers were culled from student papers during my last few years of teaching. The examples are presented for enjoyment, not for ridicule. We were all neophytes once, so there won't be a single reader among us who doesn't have empathy for the offenders. After all, the more we write or make public presentations, the more likely our turn will come. The best we can hope for is that some Boswell isn't sitting nearby with nothing better to do.

Composition teachers are always telling college students to write about what they know, so I suppose it's no surprise that many English 101 essays concern the libido.

One student wrote,
"A man gets very wick in the knees when he sees a beautiful woman." Perhaps he was trying out a variation on the venerable moth-and-candle-flame analogy.

To overcome his shyness, he might try the method advocated by a classmate:

"I want a TV program to be entertaining first of all, and then have a massage if one can be worked in." Not a bad idea; some of those commercials are interminable.

A young woman suggested, **"I feel if you are going to have sex with your boyfriend or your husband you should use some kind of conception."** That may be the very reason one of her classmates warned, **"Many young girls are getting pregnant every day."** You'd think they'd learn the first day, wouldn't you?

If we want to take a more optimistic view, we'll find it in this reassurance: **"No one was engendered in the accident."**

One woman told of a ne'er-do-well who was **"always praying on the young ladies in the neighborhood."** Nothing like sharing an *Our Father* with a chick; it makes for a religious experience.

Of course, sometimes pregnancy is desirable, as this student observed: **"Women all over the country realize that to give birth to a child is their prim desire before they get past the age of reproduction."** Well, I'm sorry to be the one to tell you, ma'am, but you're going to have to drop your propriety at least once.

The subject of patriotism received its share of attention, too. One student lamented, **"We take our country for granite."** On the other hand, given all those recent earthquakes, it's difficult *not* to pay attention to those tectonic plates, isn't it?

Referring to an age-old custom, another student reminded us that, **"When a public official dies, the flag hangs at half mass."** I wonder if that also applies when the politician isn't Catholic.

"Teach your children the Stars Spanish Banner" was a fervent exhortation found in another paper, though monolinguists will surely take exception.

And then there was the young man who thought that it was time to slow things down a bit when he wrote, "**We can show our patriotism by flying the flag on holidays and by reading the Deceleration of Independence.**"

Of course, nothing puts a damper on patriotism more than "**politicians who use smoking mirrors,**" as one young lady complained. They are a pane, actually.

"**These factory buildings are invested with rats**" is not a line item I'd like to find in *my* retirement portfolio, but it indicates another category of concern for freshman writers: the workplace.

Complaining about her grocery store colleagues, one student wrote, "**The employees were arguing and using vaguer language.**" Actually, it hurts even more when they get specific, so things could be worse.

I don't recall what industry the following student worked in, but it was obviously dangerous: "**I was sitting at my station when something like a bulk of lightning hit me.**" That had to hurt.

It also hurts when you feel powerless at work, as this young man complained: "**I was the lowest person on the toll poll.**" That's something he'd better take up with the Road Authority or the Board of Elections.

Referring to a co-worker, one young lady confided, "**Sharon has a quick temple; you don't want to get in her way.**" I know what you mean; those pillars across the head can really smart.

Another woman shared her secret for dealing with an irate boss: "**As my preacher always says, a soft dancer turns away wrath.**" You bet—those foot stompin' dancers really drive them into a frenzy.

Managers are every worker's headache, as this student indicated: "**They will always criticize you, but they may beat around the brush to avoid a discrimination suit.**" No doubt they sweep things under the rug, too.

We have always been told crime doesn't pay, but one student claimed that, "**A person who murders and gets a life term will just come up for payroll and be on the loose again**." Sadly, that sounds unfairly profitable to me.

Another writer lamented, "**Every time you pick up a newspaper or turn on your TV or radio, someone is killed**." Good heavens — don't touch that dial! Siding with those who advocate owning a gun for self-protection, one woman wrote, "**At least with a gun you have a frightening chance**." Amen to that, sister.

One writer thought she had a surefire solution to juvenile delinquency: "**If you make your kids tow the line, they won't get into trouble**." I wonder if that line was attached to a barge.

Speaking of crackheads in his neighborhood, another writer warned, "**These people will robe you to support their habit**." I don't suppose they leave a mint on your pillow, though.

But there may be hope on the horizon, according to this essayist: "**Prisons should make some people thank twice before doing wrong**." Let's have another big *Amen!* from the choir for that one.

But the quote that has stayed with me for years, the one that haunts me on those long winter nights when I stare into the fireplace searching for the meaning of life, is this deliciously subtle one: "**My arms are slender, with just enough hair on them to be unnoticeable**." For me, that ranks right up there with the sound of one hand clapping.

The Sound and the Fury

The word *blooper* is an example of onomatopoeia [ah'-nuh-ma'-tuh-PEE-uh]. This intimidating word breaks down into two Greek roots: *onomat-*, name, and *poiein-*, to make. It denotes a word-making process in which a thing or action is represented by an imitation of the sound that it makes. In other words, the very sound of the word suggests the sense.

Even though this isn't the principal way that words come into our language, there are quite a few such words in daily use. They tend to be monosyllabic, many of them represent body noises—human or animal—and they are certainly evocative and descriptive. They're *fun* words. Here are some representatives. No doubt you'll be able to come up with many more.

babble	cackle	creak	moo
rustle	tweet	bam	cheep
ding	mumble	shush	whack
bang	chunk	flap	neigh
slap	whisk	beep	clank
gargle	oink	snicker	bobolink
clink	giggle	ping	squeak
whirr	bobwhite	clunk	gobble
splat	throb	whiz	bong
coo	grunt	plink	toot
yip	burp	cough	huff
quack	towhee	zing	whippoorwill

Many people have commented that *onomatopoeia*, rather than sounding like what it is, sounds like a urinary tract infection.

NAUTICAL OR NICE

The metaphors and other figures of speech that we use are inevitably influenced by our culture and by society's level of development. Take the human brain, for instance, and the changing nature of the metaphors that described it over the centuries. Early physicians saw it as a hydraulic system—a series of canals through which liquid was directed in order to make the limbs function. When electricity was discovered, the brain was seen as an organ that sent out electrical impulses; it was the galvanic battery that ran the system. With the Industrial Revolution, nothing would work except to imagine the brain as a machine that controlled its outlying parts by pistons and levers. In our day, the brain is just like a computer—a central processing unit that makes the various software programs run.

With all of the travel options available to us today, it is easy for us to forget the enormous impact that ships once had on history and on language. From ancient times, the nautical experience has been woven into other venues as a convenient reference point, a means of tapping into a common experience. In English, the 16th to the 19th centuries were a particularly prolific time for nautical figures of speech. Once the Spanish Armada and Portuguese competition had been dealt with, Britannia ruled the waves. All the way through the formation and solidification of the far-flung British Empire, ships were a lifeline, and their operations were important to people. Words and phrases that had a literal meaning to the crew of a ship were embraced by the non-seafaring public as a colorful way to express ideas. Sometimes, in fact, civilians had no idea that they were reflecting shipboard jargon, and that will increase as ships fade in importance, to be replaced by other technologies.

But for a moment, let's return to those days of yesteryear and remind ourselves that we still preserve figures of speech that were born on the high seas. The list is merely a sampling, but it contains figures still in common use.

all washed up: *ruined; a has-been*
When a ship ran aground, it was washed up or beached. The crew no longer had a purpose, outside of the obligation to survive.

all wracked up: *very badly damaged or destroyed*
The English word wrack derives from a Dutch word meaning a shipwreck.

aloof: *reserved; stand-offish*
Loof was the windward direction. Stand aloof was an order to keep the ship's head to the wind, an action that could help a vessel stay clear of shore or hazard—keep it at a distance.

anchor: *source of stability or security; also, a news host*
The figurative senses above come from a ship's anchor.

any port in a storm: *when the situation is intense, any relief is welcome.*
Voyages had a specific destination, and the captain was determined and obligated to arrive there, but in a storm, any shelter was a blessing.

average: *typical or usual*
The word came into English from the Old French word availe, "damage to shipping." Average came to mean the expenses distributed proportionately among ship owners, investors, and cargo owners. Mathematical average, or the mean, developed from the idea of distributing a sum among a number of people.

awning: *roof-like canvas or plastic sheltering cover over doors, windows, etc.*
The original awning seems to have first appeared on ships—a roof-like covering of canvas used as a shelter from sun or rain above the deck of a vessel.

barge in: *to intrude or interrupt in a rude manner*
A barge was a large, long, and usually unpowered flat-bottomed boat. Barges had to be pushed or pulled, and they frequently collided with other craft or with canal banks. British schoolboys applied the term to bumping or jostling one another in high spirits. From there, it developed into butting in.

batten down the hatches: *get ready for trouble*
The battens were strips of wood strategically nailed to spars and masts. As a storm approached, hatches were secured by ropes, and tarps were tied and battened over large openings.

be all at sea: *confused*
Losing your bearings while at sea puts you in the middle of nowhere, with no idea of where to go.

between the devil and the deep blue sea: *a choice between two evils*
The devil was the long seam in the planking on the waterline. Periodically, it had to be caulked, which resulted in sailors being suspended in slings between that seam and the ocean below, a precarious position.

bilge*: nonsense; sometimes a euphemism for bullshit*
The bilge was the lowest inner part of a ship's hull. Water would seep in there and eventually go quite foul. Bilge water was removed by the use of bilge pumps.

bitter end: *the last extremity, the conclusion of a tough battle or difficult situation*
"The bitter end" is that part of the chain or anchor cable that is secured inside the vessel and is seldom used. A bitt was a strong post, part of a pair, used for fastening cables. "The Bitter's end is that part of the cable doth stay within board." [Captain Smith's *Seaman's Grammar*, 1627]

booby hatch: *slang for a mental institution*
In the 18th century, the booby was a wooden hood placed over the hatch or staircase of the master's cabin in a merchant ship. Much earlier, in medieval galleys, it was a covering over a pantry

or storeroom. Perhaps it doubled as a place of confinement. In the 18th century, *booby hatch* was also slang for the police wagon that carried prisoners to jail, so it is a competing source.

broad in the beam: *wide-hipped*
The beam was the breadth of a ship at its widest point.

by and large: *generally speaking; on the whole*
Picture a compass face—a large circle. Now draw a line through it from north to south. If the wind was blowing from any point in the half-circle eastward of the line from north to south, from nearer the stern, the ship was said to be sailing *large*.
Now to some extent, sailing ships were able to make progress <u>into</u> the wind, that is, with it blowing from forward of the beam. In such cases, the ship was said to be sailing *by the wind*, *by* here having the sense of "towards".
So, *by and large* referred to all possible points of sailing.

by the board: *moot or abandoned (plan)*
To go by the board is related to "man overboard!" The board is the side of the ship, and if you fall over the side of the ship you are swept away, gone forever. The figurative use of this phrase—a lost opportunity—goes back to 1855.

came through with flying colors: *won a victory*
A 17th century term which refers to the custom of raising the flags high before sailing into port to signal victory to onlookers.

chart a new course: *prepare to set off in a new direction (as a business plan)*
The chart was a map showing coastlines, water depths, and other information that navigators needed.

clean bill of health: *to have passed a rigorous inspection*
This term has its origins in the document issued to a ship showing that the port it sailed from suffered from no epidemic or infection at the time of departure. Otherwise, there would be a foul bill of health, and receiving ports might refuse entry.

clear the decks: *prepare for action by paring to essentials*
Particularly before a battle, sailors were ordered to tie things down and remove extraneous items that might get in the way or cause injuries.

close quarters: *crowded; cramped and confining*
Not only did this describe the living arrangements for the ordinary seaman, but on warships, wooden barriers were erected at various places along the deck. When the enemy boarded, crew members in that sector would scoot behind the barrier and fire through the loopholes. Thus, they were fighting in close quarters—in close contact with the enemy.

coast is clear, the: *it's safe to proceed*
The use of this phrase in the 16th century seems to have had two meanings: (1) We have cleared the coast; we are safely at sea. (2) It may also have been a reference to smuggling operations and the absence of pesky authorities.

cut and run: *make a hasty departure*
When the need for fast action was anticipated, sails were secured to the yards with light rope that could be cut to let the canvas fall quickly to effect an escape. A less likely explanation is that in a desperate situation when escape was vital, the captain could order the anchor cable to be cut rather than go through the slower process of hauling it in.

cut of his jib, I don't like: *to dislike someone's appearance or manner*
The jib is a triangular foresail, and sailors could identify a ship's nationality by the precise shape of the jib.

deck: *a pack of cards*
Probably given this name because they were stacked like the decks of a ship.

don't give up the ship: *be steadfast; hold to your duties*
Giving up the ship was allowing the enemy to capture it during combat.

down the hatch: *a reference to drinking; also used as a crude toast*
A hatch is an opening in a ship's deck through which cargo is loaded or through which humans can embark. It didn't take much imagination to transfer the word to the mouth. The first hatch/mouth metaphors were warnings to think before you speak. By the 20th century, it referred to drinking.

figurehead: *nominal leader with little actual power*
The figurehead was the carved figure on the prow of a ship.

flagship: *the chief entity of a related group (newspaper chain, department store, etc.)*
In a fleet, the flagship was the one bearing the admiral's flag.

from stem to stern: *entirely*
The stem is at the front of a ship and the stern is at the back end.

galoot: *clumsy or uncouth person*
Sailors on warships that transported soldiers and marines to the battle scene referred to their nonworking passengers with this contemptuous term. Some say it came from the Spanish *galeoto*, a galley slave. A more colorful explanation has it coming from the Dutch *kloot*, scrotum.

get/lose your bearings: *find/lose your position, your exact location*
Bearings were determined by using a compass or by celestial reckoning.

give a wide berth to someone: *avoid someone (in a foul mood)*
Berth was sufficient space for a ship to maneuver. Wide berth meant giving more than enough room as a safety measure. **To steer clear** is an allied phrase.

go overboard: *overreact to something; go to extremes*
Overboard means going over the side of a ship, an extreme and life-threatening measure.

groggy: *dazed and unsteady*
Grog is watered-down rum. British Admiral Edward Vernon ordered the practice in the 19th century aboard British vessels. Undiluted rum was a problem for a number of reasons, but the order was not popular. Vernon's nickname was *Old Grog* because he always wore a grogram coat (a coarse fabric made of a blend of silk, mohair, and wool). It was a small step for crews to name his concoction *grog*.

hard and fast: *strict and rigid, as a rule*
A ship that has run aground is hard aground and fixed fast, in the sense of firmly in place.

headway: *progress (making headway)*
Nautically, this was a shortened version of ahead way, and signified motion forward or rate of progress (1748).

high and dry: *left in an awkward situation*
A ship that is in the yard for repair or for storage is high and dry.

in the doldrums: *depressed; inactive*
The doldrums was a region of the ocean near the equator that was noted for lack of winds, thus becalming sailing ships.

in the offing: *soon to occur*
In nautical terminology, the *offing* was the more distant part of the sea as seen from the shore, especially the deep waters that offered no anchoring ground.

junk: *useless waste*
The original meaning of junk was quite specific and nautical: old cable or rope, which could still be put to use by inventive sailors. In time, the meaning was extended beyond ship residue and came to mean useless leftovers.

jury-rig: *to slap something together for temporary emergency use.*
This referred to improvised rigging on a ship, and it developed from *jury-mast*, a temporary mast put in place of one broken or blown away. The 'jury" part probably comes from the Old French *ajurie*, help or relief.

learn the ropes: *to apprentice; to be trained in a skill*
Cadets had to learn how to tie various knots, how to identify which line controlled which sail, and how to maintain the rigging. When experienced, when someone had *shown them the ropes*, they were said to *know the ropes*.

leeway: *a margin of freedom or variation*
This was the distance a ship was forced sideways from the intended course by the action of the wind or the swelling seas.

left stranded: *helpless; in a difficult position*
A strand is a beach, especially the section between tide marks. A ship was stranded when it ran ashore.

lifeline: *anyone or anything that a person depends on in a serious situation*
Ropes or wires rigged about the ship kept crew members from being swept into the sea during a storm.

loose cannon: *a grave and unpredictable hazard; a person who behaves erratically and may cause harm.*
If a cannon tore loose from its mountings during a storm or a fierce battle, it could injure crew members as it careened about, or it could even damage and sink the ship.

loose ends: *unresolved problems or difficulties, especially at the end of a process*
Unattached ropes could not do the job for which they were intended. Tying them up or joining loose ends made things work properly.

lower the boom: *to crack down; to suddenly repress an action*
The boom is a long spar that extends from the mast to hold the foot of the sail. If the wind is strong or erratic, an unwary sailor can be struck by the boom, bringing everything to a halt. But an alternative explanation says that the boom involved in this saying is the long pole extended upwards at an angle from a derrick to hoist or lower cargo through the hatch.

lurch: *an unsteady, staggering step*
A lurch was a sudden violent roll to leeward, the result of high seas.

mainstay: *chief support (often economic)*
Our metaphorical sense comes from a stay (strong rope) that extended from the main-top to the foot of the foremast to act as support.

nausea: *an inclination to vomit; seasickness*
The Greek word ναῦς (naus) meant ship.

on an even keel: *stable; well-balanced*
The keel is the core structural member of a ship, running the entire length. When a ship rides flat on the water, tilting neither left nor right, it is on an even keel.

opportune: *favorable*
The word comes from the Latin phrase, *ob portum veniens,* meaning a wind blowing in toward a *portus*—a harbor.

overhaul: *examine or dismantle to make repairs*
When rigging was pulled apart for inspection, it was overhauled—the hoisting rope was pulled in the opposite direction to cause slack.

pipe down: *be quiet*
The bosun (boatswain) was the petty officer in charge of the deck. One of his duties was to send signals to the crew by piping on his whistle. When he "piped down," he was ordering the crew to cease activity and go to their quarters below. It was the last whistle of the day.

run afoul of: *in conflict; in trouble with*
When shrouds or ropes entangled, they were afoul.

run a tight ship: *be in control*
A "tight" ship was neat and trim both in appearance and in its management.

scuttlebutt: *gossip; rumor*
A butt was a covered wooden cask used to store drinking water. The scuttle was the opening on top through which a cup or ladle could be inserted. Sailors who gathered around for a refreshing drink of water acted much like office mates who huddle around the water cooler today: stories fly and reputations die.

show your true colors: *reveal who you really are*
Warships carried flags from many nations in order to lure opponents into firing range. The rules of civilized engagement required the captain to run his actual national flag up the pole before firing a shot.

single-handedly: *without help; unassisted*
A hand is a crew member (*all hands on deck*). To single-hand is to sail a boat alone.

stand by: v. *wait;* n. *passenger without a reservation waiting for a seat*
As a verb, *stand by* was a naval order (1699) to keep the ship in readiness and on watch. A century and a quarter later, as a noun it described a vessel kept nearby for emergencies.

strike one's colors: *give up*
"Colors" was a term for the flag. To strike them was to lower them, to totally remove them as a sign of surrender. The victory was timed from that moment, and international law forbade either vessel to fire upon the other after the colors were struck.

take a different tack: *try a different approach*
"To tack" means to bring a vessel into the wind in order to change course. To facilitate this, a rope is attached to the corner of a sail, and it has been called the tack since 1481. Tack also represents the direction in which the ship is going. All of this eventually led to the figurative sense of "a course or line of conduct or action." Let's hope we are never on the wrong tack.

take over the helm: *take charge*
The helm of a ship is its tiller or wheel, so the person who does the steering is in a position of control.

take someone down a peg or two: *to humble someone*
A ship's colors (flag) were fastened by means of pegs. The higher the colors were flown, the greater the rank. When someone of lesser rank took over a vessel, his flag had to be installed in a lower position than the last commander's.

take the wind out of someone's sails: *to stop someone in her tracks*
If an enemy ship sailed to the windward side of another ship, it would block the wind, and the sails on the affected ship would slacken as they were deprived of the breeze.

taken aback: *caught by surprise; stopped in one's tracks*
A sail is aback when it serves to drive a ship in the direction of the stern. There is no forward motion.

three sheets to the wind: *intoxicated*
The sheet is a rope that holds the sail. If the sheet flaps in the wind, unattached, the sail will flap and behave erratically, causing the vessel to totter back and forth like a drunk attempting to walk.

toe the line: *obey the rules; conform*
The space between deck planks was filled with oakum (loose hemp or jute fiber), then sealed with pitch. As a result, dark parallel lines ran the length of the deck. When the crew was required to line up in formation for inspection or instructions, they would place the toes of their boots on these lines to achieve a neat formation. Variations included *toe the mark* and *toe the crack*.

turn a blind eye to: *to deliberately ignore a message or situation*
In 1801, during the siege of Copenhagen, the flagship sent out a signal to withdraw. Lord Horatio Nelson, second in command, had no intention of following the order, so he held his glass to his blind eye and boldly declared that he could see no signal to retreat. The British went on to win a critical victory over the French.

weather the storm: *to get through difficult times*
This refers to a ship making it through a tumultuous storm. "Weather" here is shorthand for *survive the effects of the weather.*

weigh: *to ponder or consider; also, to determine the heaviness of something*
The original sense of the word was "a lifting motion" or "carrying," as in *to weigh anchor.*

we're all in the same boat: *to be in similar circumstances*
Crew members at sea are locked into a common environment. They share the same hardships and the same fate, so they have to work together.

The creation of nautical metaphors may have slowed down in our day, but they have not disappeared altogether. Several times recently, in the context of the financial market and of real estate values, I have heard commentators using the phrase, "the perfect storm." It refers to an incident in 1991 in the North Atlantic, during which intense weather forces came together in an unprecedented way and formed a scenario of disaster for commercial fishermen. Metaphorically, market forces on Wall Street and housing prices and availability are vulnerable to intense negative forces—vulnerable to the perfect storm. Man overboard!

NIFTY NEOLOGISMS

I have always been intrigued by offbeat words, especially those excruciatingly specific nouns that fill a void I never knew was there.

Need a word for the fine wood powder left by boring insects? Of course you do; try frass. What about that indentation at the bottom of a wine bottle? It's called a punt. Crossword puzzle fans all know that an aglet is the plastic or metal sheath at the tip of a shoelace. And who would have thought that the world needed a word like haw, a dog's inner eyelid.

Occasionally, however, I cannot find a word with the specific meaning that I need. It is then that I turn to Greek and Latin word parts and invent a term. It may never catch on with the general public, but it gives me a sound to mutter as I think or write about the subject. After all, philosophers warn us that something that cannot be named may not even exist.

Allow me to share some of my recent neologisms. I guarantee that you never knew you might need them.

kerysomnia *n.* The unfailing ability to fall asleep during a sermon. [< Gr *keryssein,* to proclaim, + L *somnus,* sleep]

synchrotenation *n.* That embarrassing moment at the family dinner table when everyone reaches for the last pork chop at the same time. [< E *synchro-,* simultaneously, + L *tenere,* to take hold of]

anamelophobia *n.* Fear of, or aversion to, elevator music. [<Gr ana, upward, + melo, music, + phob, fear]

optotoxicidal adj. for pertaining to poisonous looks that could kill, especially from a spouse. [<Gr ops, eye, + toxikon, poison, + E-cide, to kill]

umbalgia n. The excruciating pain experienced when a doorknob violently strikes one's thigh. [<L umbo, a knob or projection + -algia, pain]

vinigrate v. -grated, -grating To annoy others while under the influence of alcoholic beverages. [<L vinum, wine + grate, to annoy]

coprovore n. A subordinate who is forced to listen without interruption as his or her boss engages in unrelenting verbal abuse. [<Gr kopro-, dung, + L vorare, eat]

vellicitude (vel-ISS-uh-tewd) n. Having one's sleeve plucked by a persistent street beggar. [<L vellicare, to pull or pluck]

philatelicide n. 1. A postal worker who goes on a rampage and murders his co-workers. 2. The act of a philatelicide. [<G philately, the study of stamps, + L -cide, murder]

pisced-off (pisht-OFF) adj. Angry because the market is out of fresh fish. [<L. piscis, fish, + -off]

proctotious (prok-TOE-shuss) adj. Of or pertaining to a lazy knave, as one's brother-in-law. [<Gr proctos, rectum, + L otium, leisure]

frustrum *n.*, pl. **frustra**. An unendurably itchy spot in the middle of one's back which defies all efforts to reach it. [<L *frustra* in vain]

mephitomint *n.*, pl. **-mints**. A lozenge deliberately designed to produce foul breath in certain social situations, such as a blind date that is going badly. [<L *mephitis*, noxious stench, + *mint*]

testiculate *v.* To make an obscene gesture by grabbing one's crotch. [<L *testis,* testicle]

ructitude *n.* The satisfying feeling of relief which comes after a particularly good belch. [< L *eructare,* to belch]

rhinothetic *adj.* Having the tendency to stick one's nose in other people's business. [< Gr *rhin-,* nose, + E -*thetic* > Gr-*tithenai,* to put or place]

bisedilious *adj.* Pertaining to a bus rider or theatergoer so large that two seats are necessary to accommodate him or her— and who invariably sits next to you. [<L *bi-,* two, + *sedile,* seat]

podostomatic *adj.* Tending to suffer from foot-in-mouth disease. [< Gr *pod-,* foot, + *stom-,* mouth]

bufogamation (bew-FOE-guh-MAY'-shun) *n.* The act of marrying a prince only to discover that he's really a toad. [<Gr *bufo-* toad, + *gam-,* wed]

pharmasuitical *adj.* Pertaining to a multi-pocketed garment worn by drug smugglers. [< Gr *pharmako,* drug, + Eng. *suit*]

pharanoia *n.* A psychosis characterized by the delusion that one is a lighthouse keeper. [< Gr *pharos,* lighthouse, + -*noia* < *nous,* mind]

ecollegey *n.* The acquisition of advanced degrees via the internet. [blend of *ecology* and *college*]

Finally, for my fellow golfers, a few terms to elevate the experience beyond four-letter words.

dendrotropic: pertaining to a golf ball that insists on going into the woods.

hydrotropic: pertaining to a golf ball that insists on going into the water hazard.

psammotropic: pertaining to a golf ball that insists on going into the sand trap.

graminotropic: pertaining to the extremely rare golf ball that lands in the fairway. [Gr *tropos*, attracted to; *dendr-* tree; *hydr-* water; *psamm-* sand; *gramin-* grass]

Word, Bro.

KRAZY KOMBOS

Do you have time on your hands? Do you ever suffer from insomnia? Do you get snowed in during the winter? Are you about to take an interminable coast-to-coast flight?

If you answered yes to any of the above, I've got a diversion for you. I call it Kombos, and it comes in as many flavors as you have imagination: Business Kombos, Song Kombos, Movie Kombos, Law Firm Kombos, etc.

Let's use Business Kombos as an example. In this version, you combine elements of company names—the more bizarre the end product, the better.

Here's an example: what do you get when you combine Beacon Blankets + Bear Sterns + Ansell Protective Products?
Answer: Protective Bear Blankets.

Or what do you get when you combine Dayton Superior + Cooper Tire & Rubber + Cutler-Hammer?
Answer: Superior Rubber Hammer

There are only three rules. First, the company or industry names must be authentic. You might want to cull them from *The Wall Street Journal* or go on line to get a list of the Fortune 500 or some other listing of corporations.

Second, you are allowed an –*s* wildcard. The –*s* can be added to a 3rd person singular verb to make it singular, or it may be added to a noun to make it plural. (Ah, the paradox of language!) For instance, you could add it to the second example above to produce

Superior Rubber Hammers. Or, in Fruit of the Loom + Leech Tool & Die = Fruit Die, the verb would agree only if you added an –s: Fruit Dies.

Finally, you may add punctuation—especially a comma or a colon—if it enhances the sentence. Let the game begin.

Sample:

Good Year Tire
   +Apple Computer
   +Direct TV
   +Headstrong Corporation
   +IBM Computer
   +Johnson Control
= Good Computers Direct; Headstrong Computers Control

BUSINESS KOMBOS [Warning: not necessarily in sequential order]

(1) Dresser
   + Cross Creek Apparel
   +Tingley Rubber Corporation
   +Sharp

= _____

(2) Fawn Industries
   + Hunter Sadler
   + Pay-Pal
   + Price Waterhouse

= _____

(3) American Uniform Company
   +Sapient
   + Fellowes
   + Ernst & Young
   + Dayton Superior
   + Cadence Design Systems

= _____

(4) Quaker Oats
+ Qwest
+ United Technologies
+ World Kitchen

= _____

(5) Linens N Things
+ Johnson's Wrecker Service
+ Johnson's Controls
+ Beacon Blankets
+ Home Depot

= _____

(6) Art Leather Manufacturing
+ Hyper Tech Solutions
+ Merit Abrasive Products
+ Discover
+ The Underwear Corporation

= _____

(7) Hamilton Beach
+ Sights Denim Systems
+ Sweetheart Cup Co.
+ Respiratory Support Products
+ Bard Access Systems

= _____

(8) John Deere
+Headstrong Corporation
+ Bard Access Systems
+ Sears Roe-Buck
+ Waste Management

= _____

(9) Target
+ Dairy Queen
+ Regal Rugs
+ Sweetheart Cup Company
+ Crown Holdings

= _____

(10) Crown Holdings
+ Good-Rich Tires
+ Family Dollar Stores
+ Concise Fabricators
+Procter & Gamble
+Bed Bath & Beyond

= _____

ANSWERS

(1) Sharp Cross Dresser Rubber Apparel
(2) Fawn Hunters Pay Price
(3) Sapient Young Fellowes Design Superior Uniforms
(4) Quaker Qwest: United World
(5) Home Wrecker Controls Blankets N Linens
(6) Discover Hyper Abrasive Leather Underwear
(7) Beach Sights: Cup Support Systems
(8) Headstrong Deere Bucks Management Systems
(9) Queen Sweetheart Targets Regal Crown
(10) Rich Fabricators Gamble Dollars Beyond Holdings

(If you have better answers, more power to you!)

MOVIE KOMBOS

American Film Institute: the 100 greatest American movies of all time.

1. CITIZEN KANE (1941)
2. CASABLANCA (1942)
3. THE GODFATHER (1972)
4. GONE WITH THE WIND (1939)
5. LAWRENCE OF ARABIA (1962)
6. THE WIZARD OF OZ (1939)
7. THE GRADUATE (1967)
8. ON THE WATERFRONT (1954)
9. SCHINDLER'S LIST (1993)
10. SINGIN' IN THE RAIN (1952)
11. IT'S A WONDERFUL LIFE (1946)
12. SUNSET BOULEVARD (1950)
13. THE BRIDGE ON THE RIVER KWAI (1957)
14. SOME LIKE IT HOT (1959)
15. STAR WARS (1977)
16. ALL ABOUT EVE (1950)
17. THE AFRICAN QUEEN (1951)
18. PSYCHO (1960)
19. CHINATOWN (1974)
20. ONE FLEW OVER THE CUCKOO'S NEST (1975)
21. THE GRAPES OF WRATH (1940)
22. 2001: A SPACE ODYSSEY (1968)
23. THE MALTESE FALCON (1941)
24. RAGING BULL (1980)
25. E.T. THE EXTRA-TERRESTRIAL (1982)
26. DR. STRANGELOVE (1964)
27. BONNIE AND CLYDE (1967)
28. APOCALYPSE NOW (1979)
29. MR. SMITH GOES TO WASHINGTON (1939)
30. THE TREASURE OF THE SIERRA MADRE (1948)
31. ANNIE HALL (1977)
32. THE GODFATHER PART II (1974)
33. HIGH NOON (1952)
34. TO KILL A MOCKINGBIRD (1962)
35. IT HAPPENED ONE NIGHT (1934)
36. MIDNIGHT COWBOY (1969)

37. THE BEST YEARS OF OUR LIVES (1946)
38. DOUBLE INDEMNITY (1944)
39. DOCTOR ZHIVAGO (1965)
40. NORTH BY NORTHWEST (1959)
41. WEST SIDE STORY (1961)
42. REAR WINDOW (1954)
43. KING KONG (1933)
44. THE BIRTH OF A NATION (1915)
45. A STREETCAR NAMED DESIRE (1951)
46. A CLOCKWORK ORANGE (1971)
47. TAXI DRIVER (1976)
48. JAWS (1975
49. SNOW WHITE AND THE SEVEN DWARFS (1937)
50. BUTCH CASSIDY AND THE SUNDANCE KID (1969)
51. THE PHILADELPHIA STORY (1940)
52. FROM HERE TO ETERNITY (1953)
53. AMADEUS (1984)
54. ALL QUIET ON THE WESTERN FRONT (1930)
55. THE SOUND OF MUSIC (1965)
56. M*A*S*H (1970)
57. THE THIRD MAN (1949)
58. FANTASIA (1940)
59. REBEL WITHOUT A CAUSE (1955)
60. RAIDERS OF THE LOST ARK (1981)
61. VERTIGO (1958)
62. TOOTSIE (1982)
63. STAGECOACH (1939)
64. CLOSE ENCOUNTERS OF THE THIRD KIND (1977)
65. THE SILENCE OF THE LAMBS (1991)
66. NETWORK (1976)
67. THE MANCHURIAN CANDIDATE (1962)
68. AN AMERICAN IN PARIS (1951)
69. SHANE (1953)
70. THE FRENCH CONNECTION (1971)
71. FORREST GUMP (1994)
72. BEN-HUR (1959)
73. WUTHERING HEIGHTS (1939)
74. THE GOLD RUSH (1925)
75. DANCES WITH WOLVES (1990)
76. CITY LIGHTS (1931)
77. AMERICAN GRAFFITI (1973)

78. ROCKY (1976)
79. THE DEER HUNTER (1978)
80. THE WILD BUNCH (1969)
81. MODERN TIMES (1936)
82. GIANT (1956)
83. PLATOON (1986)
84. FARGO (1996)
85. DUCK SOUP (1933)
86. MUTINY ON THE BOUNTY (1935)
87. FRANKENSTEIN (1931)
88. EASY RIDER (1969)
89. PATTON (1970)
90. THE JAZZ SINGER (1927)
91. MY FAIR LADY (1964)
92. A PLACE IN THE SUN (1951)
93. THE APARTMENT (1960)
94. GOODFELLAS (1990)
95. PULP FICTION (1994)
96. THE SEARCHERS (1956)
97. BRINGING UP BABY (1938)
98. UNFORGIVEN (1992)
99. GUESS WHO'S COMING TO DINNER (1967)
100. YANKEE DOODLE DANDY (1942)

Here's another playground, and this time you'll be in control. In 2005, The American Film Institute released its picks for the 100 greatest American movies of all time. They are listed above. Combining title elements can lead to some strange new movie marquees:

Bonnie & Clyde Go to Washington
[27 +29]
Snow White and the Quiet Wolves
[49 +54 +75]
Giant Psycho Citizen in Paris
[82 +18 +68]
Guess Who's Singin' on the Waterfront?
[99 +54 +8]
The Birth of a Graffitti Queen
[44 +10 +17]
Jaws in the Duck Soup
[48 +92 +86]
Raiders of the Extraterrestrial Apartment
[60 +25 +93]
Raging West Side Butch
[24 +41 +50]
The Sound of Bringing Up Wind
[55 +97 +4]
The Third Stagecoach Encounters Apocalypse
[57 +63 +28]
An Unforgiven Duck Hunter Named Tootsie
[98 +85 +45 +62]
Some Like Mockingbird Soup Hot
[14 +34 +85 +14]
All About Midnight Mutiny Music in Arabia
[16 +36 +86 5]
Wizard Flew in Space Without a Driver
[6 +20 +10 +22 +59 +47]
Orange Dwarfs Without Vertigo
[46 +49 +59 +61]
The Wonderful Silence of the Quiet Candidate
[11 +65 +54 +67]
Duck Pulp Without Grapes
[85 +95 +59 +21]

White Godfather Goes African
[49 +3 +29 +17]
Hunter Lambs Kill Citizen on Boulevard
[29 +65 +34 +1 +12]
The Sound of Music in the Close Rear Apartment
[55 +10 +64 +42 +93]

I'm sure that you'll do a lot better than this. If you wish to share your creations, please ship them along to wordmall@aol.com

SIGNIFICANTLY INSIGNIFICANT

There are many reasons why people punch up the perceived insignificance of others. Sometimes it's based on a rigid social system; if there is no pup at the bottom of the pile, how can there be a top dog? Sometimes it's a cheap weapon for self-aggrandizement; if I can make someone count for nothing, then *my* value allegedly goes up. Sometimes it's a cruel weapon, a means of hurting someone because of a perceived slight or wrong. Unfortunately, whatever the motive, it is a common practice. Consequently, there are available to us dozens of figures of speech to highlight insignificance.

Take, for instance, the familiar sequence, *"you're not the only…"* To cite just a few examples, we have

- You're not the only bullet in the clip
- You're not the only car on the freeway
- You're not the only chip in the bag
- You're not the only train left out in the rain
- You're not the only fish in the sea
- You're not the only oyster in the stew
- You're not the only pea in the pod
- You're not the only sandwich in the deli
- You're not the only pebble on the beach
- You're not the only star in the sky

Of course, this has a serious rival in the *"not worth a/the ..."* sequence.

- Not worth a button
- Not worth a curse
- Not worth a fig leaf
- Not worth a hair
- Not worth a hill of beans
- Not worth an iota
- Not worth a pickle
- Not worth a pit stop
- Not worth a rat's ass
- Not worth a second look
- Not worth a second thought
- Not worth a shrug
- Not worth a sniff
- Not worth a straw
- Not worth a tin whistle
- Not worth a tinker's damn
- Not worth the effort
- Not worth the paper it's printed on
- Not worth the price of admission
- Not worth the price of a bullet
- Not worth the time or trouble

But popular as all those are, they take second place to their more poetic brethren, the metaphors and allusions that hint broadly at insignificance. Let's remind ourselves of a few.

beautiful downtown Burbank: *sarcastic put down of a town.*
This insult originated on Rowan & Martin's 1968 TV show, *Laugh-In*. It came to stand for any esthetically ugly or culturally deprived town in the U.S.

bottom of the pecking order: *lowest in the hierarchy*
Instinctively, dominant chickens peck weaker birds without fear of retaliation. An allied word is **henpecked**.

bush league: *of inferior status, second-rate*
The term sprang up when major league teams began to subsidize minor leagues as talent feeders in the early 20th century. These teams were located away from major cities, out in the bush [Dutch *bosch*, woods or forest].

chicken feed: *insignificant amount*
The grain fed to chickens in pioneer days was low in quality, something not really fit for human consumption. In addition, it was ground into very small pieces. [Watch out for a current mistake: chicken feet.]

dime a dozen: *commonplace; almost worthless*
Items that go for ten cents a dozen would be worth less than a penny apiece.

down/out in the boondocks: *in a remote rural area*
This was a slang term created by G.I.s stationed in the Philippine Islands during WWII. Most likely, it's a corruption of the Tagalog *bundok*, meaning mountain.

drop in the bucket: *absurdly small quantity in relation to the whole*
The phrase appears in *KJV, Isaiah 40:15*—"Behold, the nations are as a drop of a bucket, and are counted as the small dust of the balance."

drop in the ocean: *absurdly small quantity in relation to the whole*
This was coined in the early 1700s, probably as an enthusiastic exaggeration on the bucket image above.

featherweight/lightweight: *an insignificant person*
The terms come from two sports: horse racing and boxing. They refer to participants in a certain weight category, but they are also used pejoratively outside these sports to indicate lack of intelligence, authority, or influence.

great unwashed: *general public without influence*
These are people poor enough not to have indoor plumbing.
The phrase was used by the British in reference to the rabble of
the French Revolution.

hill of beans: *of little value; trifling*
A bean has been used since the year 1297 to designate a thing
of small value.

hoi polloi: *Greek for "the many," the masses, the great unwashed*
Since *hoi* already means "the" in Greek, don't say "THE hoi
polloi." This is a plural form, so it can't apply to an individual.

jerkwater town: *small town that is big enough for a railroad water
tank, but not big enough for a busy station*
In the late 1800s, steam engines would stop only to fill up with
water in such a location. The fireman would pull (jerk) a cord
attached to a spigot on the water tower. Variant: **tank town**

low man on the totem pole: *unimportant person*
A totem pole contains symbolic carvings on a tree trunk, one
above the other. Many are found in Alaska, British Columbia,
and northern Washington. On some totem poles, the most
important figure is on top, but there are others with that figure
at the bottom, so the phrase doesn't reflect a uniform reality.

Mickey Mouse: *cheap or inferior; worthless; childish*
This designation probably originated in the mid-1930s when
the Ingersoll Watch Company sold a popular, but not very
durable, watch for $2. It featured Mickey Mouse on its face,
and his moving arms pointed to hours and minutes.

mom and pop business: *smalltime operation*
This refers to a small business establishment, usually run by a
husband and wife team who can't afford to hire outside help.

no great shakes: *unimportant or unimpressive*
The *Oxford English Dictionary* points to gambling as the source:
a gambler who gets a low roll on the shake of the dice wins
nothing.

not worth a continental: *worthless*
A continental was paper money printed in American Revolutionary times. Even though the Continental Congress had no authority to tax before the Constitution was put into force, and even though there was no backing of any sort, millions of dollars' worth of promissory notes were issued. Eventually, they were considered worthless.

not worth a plugged nickel: *worthless*
Plugs are the holes made in coins to extract some metal which can be used for other purposes. Coins tampered with in this manner are no longer considered legal tender.

not worth a rap: *worthless*
The rap was a half-penny in use in Ireland in the early 18th century.

not worth a red cent: *worthless*
American pennies were once made with more copper; thus, they had a redder tinge than they do now.

not worth your salt: *worthless; useless*
Roman soldiers were given a *salarium*, an allotment or allowance with which to purchase salt, an essential but expensive component of their diets. A soldier who wasn't worth his salt was a slacker; he didn't earn his salary.

one-horse town: *unimportant place*
This was an extremely small, insignificant rural area with such a low population that a single shared horse could serve everyone's needs.

peanut gallery: *source of unimportant criticism*
In a theater, the peanut gallery was the section of seats farthest removed from the stage. In many theaters, peanuts were sold to the people in the least expensive seats. Since these were the cheapest seats in the house, they attracted a lower class, and often boisterous, crowd. The phrase was made famous in the fifties by the *Howdy Doody Show*. Host Buffalo Bob Smith would frequently refer to the peanut gallery, "peanut" being a pun referring to small children.

penny-ante: *small time; involving a paltry amount of money*
Originally, it was a poker game in which the ante or minimum wager was only a penny.

Podunk: *any hick town; the middle of nowhere*
The name, of Mohican origin, may refer originally either to the Podunk near Hartford, Connecticut, or to that near Worcester, Massachusetts.

run-of-the-mill: *average, common, mediocre*
Originally, it applied to lots of manufactured goods that have not been inspected, and consequently not sorted or graded for quality. A run is the period of continuous operation while the machines are producing output.

runt of the litter: *puny; small and weak*
The smallest animal in a single litter (birth) is the runt. Applied to a human, it is an insult about height or strength. The *Oxford English Dictionary* gives the word *runt* the "origin unknown" designation.

small change: *something of little value*
Small change in the American monetary system includes pennies, nickels, and dimes.

small fry: *insignificant people*
Originally, small fry were the young offspring of salmon, herring, and other fish. The Norse word *frae* meant seed. It was applied here because of the seed-like masses of eggs produced by these fish.

small potatoes: *unimportant concept; insignificant amount of money; trivial person*
One who has eaten a small potato doesn't get filled up.

tank town: *small town that is big enough for a railroad water tank, but not big enough for a busy station*
In the late 1800s, steam engines would stop simply to fill up with water. The fireman would pull (jerk) a cord attached to a spigot on the water tower. Variant: **jerkwater town**

tempest in a teapot: *great uproar over a trivial matter*

Ultimately, it dates back to Cicero's *De Legibus*—"tempest in a ladle."

work for peanuts: *earn an insignificant sum*

Peanuts are not expensive. To accept them instead of money would be the act of a powerless person.

Finally, I am indebted to my wife for providing a saying with which I was unfamiliar. She heard it as a child in Indiana: "If your brains were dynamite, you wouldn't have enough to blow your nose." A variation posted on a web site reads, "If your brains were dynamite, you wouldn't have enough to blow the wax out of your ears." Tough people, those Hoosiers.

DOUBLE YOUR PLEASURE

One is the loneliest number, and three has often been hailed as the perfect number, but there's something about the number two that resonates in our souls. To be sure, that companionable number evokes images of belonging and social bonding, but I suspect that its pervasive impact owes just as much to our centuries-old preoccupation with the medial plane, that imaginary anatomical line that runs from head to toe and divides us into right and left sides.

Consider all the pairs that cluster along that symmetrically defining line: eyes and eyebrows, ears, nostrils, cheeks, shoulders, nipples, arms, lungs, hands, buttocks, hips, legs, and feet. It's almost two too much, and it's made a major impact on our vocabulary, as a study of numerical word parts will show.

Surely, it must be more than an accident that prefixes, roots, and combining forms expressing the concept "two" outnumber all the other number parts by—well, twice as much. Let's look at some of these common and not-so-common ways of embedding the meaning "two" in words.

Word Parts Expressing "Two"

- ambi- (both)
ambidextrous: using both hands with equal facility
ambisinister: clumsy or unskillful with both hands
ambivert: personality type exhibiting both extroversion and introversion

• ambo- (both)
amboceptor: a substance that, added to another, breaks down red blood cells
ambosexous: of both sexes; hermaphrodite

• amphi- (on both sides)
amphiboly: ambiguity of speech arising from uncertain grammar
amphioxus: sharp at both ends
amphivorous: eating both animal and vegetable food

• ampho- (on both sides)
amphogenic: producing both male and female offspring
amphora: large two-handled storage jar
amphoteric: capable of functioning either as an acid or as a base

• bi- (two)
bicipital: having two heads
bifurcate: to divide or fork into two branches
bimester: a two-month period

• bin- (two)
binary: consisting of, indicating, or involving two
binate: produced or borne in pairs
binaural: having two ears

• bis- (two; twice)
bismarine: between or washed by two seas
bissextile: extra leap year day in the Julian calendar

• deutero- (second)
deuterogamy: a second marriage
Deuteronomy: 5th book of the Pentateuch, with 2nd statement of Mosaic law
deuteropathy: any abnormality secondary to another pathological condition

• deuto- (second)

deutoplasm: reserve nutritive material in the ovarian cytoplasm

deutoscolex: a secondary scolex (headlike segment of a tapeworm)

deutotergite: the second dorsal segment of the abdomen of insects

• di- (two)

dicrotic: double beat of the pulse for each beat of the heart

diplegia: paralysis of the identical part on both sides of the body

dipterous: having two winglike appendages

• dicho- (in two)

dichogamous: having male and female elements at different times

dichotic: affecting the two ears differently

dichotomous: divided or dividing into two parts

• diphy- (double)

diphycercal: having the tail divided into two equal halves

diphyletic: derived from two lines of evolutionary descent

diphyodont: developing both temporary and permanent teeth

• diplo- (two; double)

diploblastic: having two germ layers, as the embryos of sponges

diploneurous: having two nervous systems

diplopia: double vision

• disso- (double)

dissogeny: in ctenophores, two periods of sexual maturity

dissology: repetition

• double- (in combination)

double-barreled: gun having two barrels, side by side or over and under

doubleheader: two events held consecutively on the same program

double-team: to guard an opponent with two players at one time

- du- (two)

duplation: multiplication by two

duplex: having two principal elements or parts

duplicate: existing in two corresponding or identical parts

- duo- (two)

duologue: a dialogue between two persons

duopoly: an oligopoly limited to two sellers

duopsony: market condition with only two buyers

- duplicato- (doubly)

duplicato-dentate: toothed leaves in which the teeth are also dentate

duplicato-serrate: serrated leaves whose notches are themselves serrate

duplicato-ternate: leaves themselves composed of three leaves each

- duplici- (duplex)

duplicidentate: rodents having two pairs of upper incisor teeth

duplicipennate: having two wings folded longitudinally in repose

- dyo- (two)

Dyophysite: person who says that Christ has both divine and human natures

Dyothelite: person who holds that Christ has both divine and human wills

- gemelli- (twin)

gemelled: coupled; paired

gemelliparous: producing twins

gemellous: duplicated

- gemin- (double)

gemination: doubling; duplication; repetition

geminiflorous: having flowers arranged in pairs

geminous: occurring in pairs

- twi- (double)

twibill: an adz/ax combination

twi-headed: two-headed

twi-night: baseball doubleheader in which the second game ends at night

- zyga-/zygo- (pair)

zygapophysis: paired processes of the neural arch of a vertebra

zygodactyl: having the toes arranged two in front and two in back

zygomorphic: having bilateral symmetry

Obviously, when it comes to numbers, two really counts. And a list such as this is more than a mere exercise in curiosity, of course. Since prefixes, roots, combining forms, and suffixes are the stuff of verbal recycling, once we learn a word part and its meaning, we increase our vocabulary in the most painless way possible.

BAR NONE

Incongruity lies at the heart of most humor. The interplay of resemblance and opposition tickles the imagination and elicits laughter—at least from people properly equipped to discover the connection between underlying components.

Puns, which usually play on words with multiple meanings, are just as likely to elicit groans as laughter, but a groan is a grudging acknowledgement that something funny has been experienced, sort of a covert snicker. And because they play with opposing meanings, puns are a great way to experience the lighter side of language while developing a greater sensitivity to vocabulary.

I'm not sure why, but many puns and jokes take place in bars. Rather than spend time analyzing why that is and how humor works—a quick way to stifle fun—let's just open the door and walk into the nearest bar.

A pony walks into a bar and says, "Bartender, may I have a drink?"
The bartender says, "What? I can't hear you. Speak up!"
"May I please have a drink?"
"What? You'll have to speak up!"
"Could I please have a drink?"
"Now listen, if you don't speak up I won't serve you."
"I'm sorry, I'm just a little hoarse."

A pig goes into a bar and orders ten drinks. He finishes them up and the bartender says, "Don't you need to know where the bathroom is?"

The pig says, "No, I go wee wee all the way home."

A kangaroo walks into a bar. He orders a beer.

The bartender says, "That'll be $10." After a moment he leans towards the kangaroo and remarks, "You know, we don't get many kangaroos coming in here." The kangaroo says, "At $10 a beer, it's not hard to understand why."

A termite walks into a bar room and asks, "Is the bar tender here?"

A three-legged dog hobbles into a western saloon. He limps up to the bar and announces, "I'm lookin' fer the man that shot my paw."

A horse walks into a bar. The bartender says, "So, why the long face?"

A grasshopper hops into a bar. The bartender says, "You're quite a celebrity around here. We've even got a drink named after you."

The grasshopper says, "You've got a drink named Mortimer?"

A man walks into a bar and orders a beer. He sips it and sets it down. A monkey swings across the bar and urinates in the pint. The man asks the barman who owns the monkey. The barman replies, "The piano player."

The man walks over to the piano player and says, "Do you know your monkey pissed in my beer?"

The pianist replies, "No, but if you hum it, I'll play it."

A duck goes into a bar and asks the bartender, "You got any fish?"

The bartender says, "No. This is a bar and we don't sell fish," so the duck leaves.

Next day, the duck goes back to the bar and asks, "You got any fish?"

The bartender says, "I told you yesterday. This is a bar and we don't sell fish."

The following day, the duck returns and asks, "You got any fish?"

The bartender loses it, grabs the duck by the neck, and screams, "I TOLD YOU **TWICE**. THIS IS A BAR. WE DON"T SELL FISH! IF YOU ASK AGAIN, I'M GONNA NAIL YOUR *@#& WEBBED FEET TO THE FLOOR!"

The next day, the duck goes in the bar and asks, "Got any nails?"

The bartender sighs and says, "No, we don't have any nails."

The duck says, "Good. Got any fish?"

A seal walks into a bar. The bartender says, "What'll you have?"

The seal says, "Anything but Canadian Club."

A snake slithers into a bar and the bartender immediately says, "I'm sorry, but I can't serve you."

"Why not?" asks the snake.

The bartender says, "Because you can't hold your liquor."

A chicken walks into a bar.

The bartender says "We don't serve poultry!"

The chicken says "That's OK. I just want a drink."

A hamburger or sandwich walks into a bar and the bartender says, "Sorry, we don't serve food in here."

A guy walks into a bar with jumper cables wrapped around his neck. The suspicious bartender looks him over for a minute, then says, "Alright, you can come in and have a drink, but don't start anything!"

A neutron walks into a bar and orders a beer. The bartender sets the beer down.
The neutron asks, "How much?"
The bartender says, "For you, no charge!"

Two hydrogen atoms walk into a bar.
One says, "I've lost my electron."
The other says, "Are you sure?"
The first replies, "Yes, I'm positive..."

A customer was sitting in a bar having a few drinks when he noticed a tiny little spot on the wall that seemed to be moving. He called it to the bartender's attention, who glanced at it and said, "It's just a ladybug."
After a moment of stunned silence the customer said, "My goodness, what incredible eyesight you have!"

A guy walks into a bar, sits down, and hears a small voice say, "You look very nice today." He looks around, but no one's there.
A few minutes later he again hears a small voice: "That's a very nice shirt."
Puzzled, the guy asks the bartender, "Who is that speaking to me?"
The bartender says, "Oh, those are the peanuts. They're complimentary!"

A bear walks into a bar and says, "I'll have a beer and . . . . some of those peanuts."
The bartender says, "Why the big pause?"

A man walks into a bar with a slab of asphalt under his arm and says, "A beer, please, and one for the road."

William Shakespeare walks into a bar and asks the bartender for a beer.

"I can't serve you," says the bartender. "You're Bard for life!"

A man walks into a bar holding an alligator. He asks the bartender, "Do you serve lawyers here?"

The bartender says, "Yes, of course we do!"

"Good," replies the man. "Give me a beer, and I'll have a lawyer for my alligator."

Two strings walk into a bar. The first string tries to order, but the bartender throws him out and yells, "I don't serve strings in this bar!"

The other string quickly backs out the door, frizzes his surface, twists himself up, then comes back in and orders.

The bartender shouts, "Hey, didn't you hear what I told your buddy?"

The string says, "Yeah."

The bartender growls, "Well, aren't you a string?"

The string says, "No, I'm a frayed knot."

Two cartons of yogurt walk into a bar. The bartender says to them, "We don't serve your kind in here."

One of the yogurt cartons says back to him, "Why not? We're cultured individuals."

For years and years, a doctor had been having a drink after work at the same bar. Every time he walked in the door, the barman would mix his favorite drink, a hazelnut daiquiri. One day, the bartender didn't have any hazelnuts in the bar. Wondering what to do, he spied some hickory nuts and tried to make the drink with them instead. The doctor came in at his regular time, took a sip of the drink and exclaimed, "This isn't a hazelnut daiquiri!"

"No," said the bartender, "it's a hickory daiquiri, Doc."

So this guy walks into a bar, and as he makes his way to the counter, he stops and talks to everyone in the bar. As he finishes with each group of people, they all get up and leave and go stand outside the window, looking in. Finally, the bar is empty except for this guy and the bartender.

The man walks up to the counter and says to the bartender, "I bet you $500 that I can pee into a shot glass from 30 feet away, and not get any outside the glass."

The bartender thinks that this guy is a nutcase, but he wants his easy $500, so he agrees. They get out a shot glass, the bartender paces off 30 feet, and the contest begins. The man pees all over the bar. He doesn't even touch the shot glass.

When he finishes, the bartender looks at him and says, "Well, I guess you owe me $500, huh?"

The man answers, "Yeah, but it's O.K. I bet all of those people outside the window $200 apiece that I could come in here and pee all over the bar with your permission."

A man rushes into a bar, orders the four most expensive 30-year-old single malts in the house, and has the barman line them up in front of him. Then without pausing, he quickly downs each one.

"Whew," the barman remarks, "You seem to be in a hurry."

"You would be too if you had what I have," the man replies.

"Why, what do you have?" the barman asks sympathetically.

"Fifty cents."

A guy walks into a bar with a dog. "This dog is the smartest dog in the world," he says. "He can answer any question."

"Oh yeah?" says one of the patrons. "Prove it!"

The man turns to his dog, and asks, "What is over our head?" "Roof!"

"How does tree bark feel?" "Ruff!"

"Who is the greatest baseball player who ever lived?" "Ruth!"

The patrons, growing tired of the show, throw the man and his dog out of the bar. The dog then turns to the man and asks, "Should I have said DiMaggio?"

A man walks into a bar and finds a friend of his nursing a very large drink.

"Fred!" he says. "What's the matter?"

Fred slowly looks up from his drink and says, "My wife of thirty years just ran off with my best friend."

"But Fred!" exclaims the man. "I'm your best friend!"

Fred smiles and turns back to his drink. "Not any more."

A man walks into a bar with a dog. The bartender says, "Hey buddy, can't you read that sign? It says no dogs allowed! Get that mutt out of here!" The man replies, "No, I can't read the sign - I'm blind, and this is my seeing-eye dog."

The bartender is embarrassed and gives the man a beer on the house.

Later that day, the guy is telling his friend about it: "I told him I was blind and I got a free beer!"

The friend then takes his dog into the bar and sits down. The bartender approaches and says, "The sign says no dogs allowed. You'll have to leave!"

The friend says, "Sorry, I can't see the sign because I'm blind, and this is my seeing-eye dog."

The bartender sneers, "Since when do they give out Chihuahuas as seeing-eye dogs?"

The man freezes in place and says, "They gave me a Chihuahua?"

A guy walks into a bar and sits down. He starts dialing numbers like there's a telephone in his hand, then puts his palm up against his cheek and begins talking. Suspicious, the bartender walks over and tells him this is a very tough neighborhood and he doesn't need any trouble here.

The guy replies, "You don't understand. I'm very hi-tech. I had a phone installed in my hand because I was tired of carrying the cellular."

The bartender says, "Prove it."

The guy dials up a number and hands his hand to the bartender. The bartender talks into the hand and carries on a conversation.

"That's incredible!" says the bartender. "I would never have believed it!"

"Yeah", said the guy, "I can keep in touch with my broker, my wife, you name it. By the way, where is the men's room?"

The bartender directs him to the men's room.

The guy goes in and 5, 10, 20 minutes go by and he doesn't return. Fearing the worst, given the dangerous neighborhood, the bartender goes into the men's room to check on the guy. The guy is spread-eagled up against the wall. His pants are pulled down and he has a roll of toilet paper up his butt.

"Oh my god!" said the bartender. "Did they rob you? Are you hurt?"

The guy turns and says, "No, no, I'm ok. I'm just waiting for a fax."

A cowboy rode into town and stopped at a saloon for a drink. Unfortunately, the locals always had a habit of picking on strangers, which he was. When he finished his drink, he found his horse had been stolen.

He went back into the bar, handily flipped his gun into the air, caught it above his head without even looking and fired a shot into the ceiling.

"Which one of you sidewinders stole my horse?!?!?" he yelled with surprising forcefulness.

No one answered.

"Alright, I'm gonna have another beer, and if my horse ain't back outside by the time I finish, I'm gonna do what I dun in Texas! And I don't want to have to do what I dun in Texas!"

Some of the locals shifted restlessly. The man, true to his word, had another beer, walked outside, and found that his horse had been returned to the post.

He saddled up and started to ride out of town. The bartender wandered out of the bar and asked, "Say, partner, before you go... what happened in Texas?"

The cowboy turned back and said, "I had to walk home."

Sign on a bar that plays only classical music: "Gone to lunch. Bach at 1:00."

A guy walks into a bar and asks for three beers. The bartender puts them up and then watches the guy go through a strange ritual. "Happy Birthday! Happy Birthday! Happy Birthday!" Each time he says the words, he drinks a beer. Then he pays and walks out.

One year later he enters the bar again and orders the same thing. The bartender watches him go through the same ritual. Curious, he asks the man why.

"Well" the guy says, "I have a friend in Ireland and a friend in Australia. We have our birthdays on the same day. We can't be together so we have agreed that on this day we will each go into our local pub and have a round of drinks for each other. We have been doing this for 55 years."

The next year, the man comes in and asks the bartender for two beers. The bartender, a bit taken aback, places two beers in front of the guy and watches him say "Happy Birthday! Happy Birthday!"

The bartender asks "So which one died?"

"Neither one."

"But you ordered only two drinks!"

"Yeah, well, I've given up drinking."

A guy walks into a bar carrying a stuffed giraffe. He orders a drink and puts the giraffe on the next stool. He drinks up, and as he pays, he knocks the giraffe onto the floor.

The bartender says, "Hey, you can't leave that lyin' there."

And the guy says, "That's not a lion, that's a giraffe."

A man went into a bar and ordered several shots of vodka. By the time the bar was closing, he was wasted. He got up to leave and fell flat on his face. "Well, I don't want the bartender to think I'm drunk, so I'll pretend I tripped and I'll try it again." So he gets up and falls on his face. "Well, the door's not too far away; I'll just crawl." When he gets outside he thinks, "Well, I only live 4 blocks away; I can make it that far." So he stands up and falls on his face. He decides he'll try it 1 block at a time, and at every block he falls flat on his face. Finally he makes it home, stands up and falls on the bed. In the morning his wife wakes him up.

"You were drunk again last night, weren't you?"

"How did you know?"

"The bartender called. He said you left your wheelchair at the bar."

So a five-dollar bill walks into a bar.

Bartender says, "Get outta here! We don't serve your type. This is a singles bar."

Two cannibals walk into a bar and sit next to a clown. The first cannibal whacks the clown on the head and they both start dining on him.

Suddenly the second cannibal looks up and says, "Hey, does this guy taste funny to you?"

Descartes walks into a bar, and the bartender asks, "Would you like a beer?"

Descartes replies, "I think not" and *POOF* — he vanishes.

A vampire walks into a bar and asks for a large glass of A-positive blood.

The bartender looks him square in the eyes and says, "I'm sorry, but we don't serve your type here."

A bartender walks into the owner's office and jerks a thumb over his shoulder.

"I thought I had seen everything, but there's a customer out there who wants to talk to you, and he claims that he's invisible."

Not even looking up from his receipts, the boss says, "Tell him I can't see him now."

A German walks into a bar and tells the bartender to serve him two martinis.

The bartender asks, "Dry?"

The German says, "No. Zwei."

A guy walks into a bar and starts chatting with a tall, attractive blonde woman. During the course of the conversation he says, "Would you like to hear a blonde joke?"

"Well," says the girl, "I'm obviously blonde, I'm 6 feet tall without heels and I've been training in judo for the past 5 years."

Raising her voice slightly, she went on, "My roommate's blonde, she's 6 feet, 2 inches tall, has been involved in karate for 10 years, she's a black belt and has been Southern Counties Ladies' Champion for the past 3 years.

"Lastly," she shouted, "My next door neighbor is blonde, she weighs over 200 pounds, and she's a professional women's wrestler. Do you still want to tell the joke about a blonde?"

"Well, no," came the reply, "not if I've got to explain it 3 times."

Three notes walk into a bar, a C, an E-flat and a G. The bartender looks up and says that he doesn't serve minors. So the E-flat leaves and the C and G have a fifth between them.

A nun in a stained and tattered dress walks into a bar and orders a pitcher full of martinis. As she sits there gulping down drinks and spilling them on the front of her outfit, the bartender shakes his head and says, "Gee, Sister, you've really got a bad habit."

A guy walks into a bar and finds a horse behind the bar serving drinks. The guy is sitting there staring at the horse, when the horse says, "What are you staring at? Haven't you ever seen a horse serving drinks before?"

The guy says, "No, it's not that. I just never thought the parrot would sell the place."

A man is waiting for his wife to give birth.

The doctor comes in and informs the dad that his son was born without torso, arms, or legs. The son is just a head! But the dad loves his son and raises him as well as he can, with love and compassion.

After 21 years, the son is old enough for his first drink. Dad takes him to the bar, tearfully tells the son he is proud of him and orders up the biggest, strongest drink for his boy. With all the bar patrons looking on curiously and the bartender shaking his head in disbelief, the boy takes his first sip of alcohol.

Whooosh! - A torso pops out!

The bar is dead silent; then bursts into a whoop of joy. The father, shocked, begs his son to drink again. The patrons chant "Take another drink!" But the bartender still shakes his head in dismay.

Whooosh! - Two arms pop out.

The bar goes wild. The father, crying and wailing, begs his son to drink again. The patrons chant "Take another drink!" The bartender ignores the whole affair. By now the boy is getting tipsy, and with his new hands he reaches down, grabs his drink and guzzles the last of it.

Whooosh! - Two legs pop out.

The bar is in chaos. The father falls to his knees and tearfully thanks God. The boy stands up on his new legs and stumbles to the left.... then to the right.... right through the front door, into the street, where a truck runs over him and kills him instantly.

The bar falls silent. The father moans in grief.

The bartender sighs and says, "That boy should have quit while he was a head."

A distraught Frenchman is talking to his bartender about taking his own life. "If things do not get better, I am going to go in Seine."

A man walks into a bar during a raging blizzard and asks for a drink. He's the only customer that night, so the bartender starts a conversation with him.

"So, what do you do for a living?"

"I'm a nudist."

"A nudist? But you're all dressed up. Shouldn't you be naked if you're a nudist?"

"Normally you'd be correct, but I'm always clothed for the winter."

A sheep walks up to the bar, changes his mind, turns around, and starts to walk back out.

"Hey!" shouts the bartender, "ewe turns aren't allowed in here."

Two verbs walk into a bar, and one orders a triple shot.
Her companion turns to her and says, "What's wrong?"
"Oh, I dunno; I guess I'm feeling tense."

A man walks into a bar and orders a beer. His attention is drawn to a bird cage behind the bar where a dozen or so canaries are lying on the cage floor, bravely singing.
"What's that all about?" he asks the bartender.
"Oh, I should have told you when you came in. Every customer receives a free legless canary, no perches necessary."

A cat walks into a bar and orders a lime daiquiri. The bartender discovers that he's out of limes, so he substitutes lemons. He slides the glass across to the cat and covertly watches.
The cat takes a sip and lets out a wail.
Feigning ignorance, the bartender asks, "Why the sour puss?"

Sign on a bar used exclusively by witches: "Spell checker wanted."

A man cashes his paycheck at a bar. The bartender lays the money on the bar, but before the man can pick up the money, the bartender places a stalk of celery on the pile of bills.
"Why did you do that?" asks the confused customer.
"I'm garnishing your wages," replies the bartender.

They just opened a bar on the moon. The drinks are good, but the place has no atmosphere.

A bartender notices a young woman quietly sobbing at the end of the bar. Concerned, he walks over to her.
"Is anything the matter, Ma'am?"
Sniff "Yes, there is. I just learned from my gynecologist that I won't ever have another child."
"Why, that's inconceivable."

A man walks into a bar and orders a cup of coffee without cream.

The barmaid says, "I'm sorry, but we're out of cream; will you take it without milk?"

A penguin walks into a bar, goes to the counter, and asks the bartender, "Have you seen my brother?"

The bartender replies, "I don't know; what does he look like?"

A sheriff walks into a saloon, and shouts for everyone's attention.

"Has anyone seen Taffeta Tom?" he asks.

"What's he look like?" asks one shoddy-looking cowboy.

"Well," replies the Sheriff. "He wears a taffeta hat, a taffeta waistcoat, a taffeta shirt, taffeta-lined boots, taffeta pants, and a taffeta jacket."

"So what's he wanted for?" asks the same cowboy.

"Rustling," replies the Sheriff.

Two guys are sitting at a bar, chatting about dogs, and trying to out-do each other.

1st guy: "I taught my dog to read."

2nd guy: "I know. My dog told me that yesterday."

A man walks into a bar at lunchtime and orders a beer and a chicken sandwich. He takes one bite of the sandwich and gestures excitedly at the bartender to come over.

"This sandwich is terrific! It's probably the best chicken sandwich I've ever had in my entire life! How do you prepare your chicken?"

The bartender shrugs. "We simply tell them they're going to die."

A bartender is chatting with a customer, and finally gets around to asking what he does for a living.

"I make wooden bells," says the man.

After a moment's thought, the bartender says, "I don't find that very appealing."

A man wearing an eye patch clumps into a bar on his wooden leg and throws himself onto a bar stool, grasping at the bar with his metal hook for balance.

The bartender looks him over for a second and asks, "What are you—some kind of pirate?"

"Aye, that I am, matey."

"How'd you lose your leg?"

Arrgh! It was a bloody shark that caught me unaware."

"And your hand?"

"Lost it in a sword fight with another bloody pirate!"

"Your eye—what happened there?"

"Blast the luck! I was high in the crow's nest when I looked up, and a seagull passing over me crapped in my eye."

"No kidding! And that blinded you?"

"Not at all, me boy. It was the fact that the new hook had been installed only the day before."

A frog enters a bar and asks for a phone because he needs to call a cab. The bartender hands him one as the frog explains, "I was illegally parked and now I've been toad."

A man walks into a bar in Baltimore and confronts the bartender: "Do you serve crabs?"

The bartender points to a stool. "Sit down, sir. We serve everyone here."

In a small country pub, all the patrons became quite used to the pub owner's little dog being around the bar, so they were quite upset when one day the little dog died.

Everyone met to decide how they could remember the little dog. The decision was to cut off his tail and stick it up behind the bar to remind everyone of the little dog's wagging tail.

The little dog went up to heaven and was about to run through the pearly gates when he was stopped by Saint Peter, who questioned the little dog as to where he was going.

The little dog said "I have been a good dog - so I am going into heaven where I belong!".

Saint Peter replied "Heaven is a place of perfection; you can not come into heaven without a tail. Where is your tail?"

So the little dog explained what had happened back on earth, and St Peter told him to go back down to earth and retrieve his tail. The little dog protested that it was now the middle of the night on earth, but St Peter would not change his mind.

So the little dog went back down to earth and scratched on the door of the pub until the bartender who lived upstairs came down and opened the door.

"My goodness, it is the spirit of the little dog. What can I do for you?" said the bartender.

The little dog explained that he wasn't allowed into heaven without his tail, and he needed it back.

The bartender replied "I would really like to help you, but my liquor license doesn't allow me to re-tail spirits after hours!"

A man is complaining to his bartender. "I've got a real problem. Every time I go to bed, I have this irrational fear that someone is under the bed. I can't sleep any more."

"Have you thought about seeing a psychiatrist?" asks the bartender.

"Oh, sure, right away. But at the first session he told me I had to visit him once a week for a year, and each session costs $150. I can't afford that."

"I'll tell you what," said the bartender. "Give me $20 and I'll provide you with a perfect solution."

The man thinks about it for a minute, then reaches for his wallet. "You're on," he says. "What's the perfect solution?"

The bartender reaches out and takes the $20 bill. "Saw the legs off your bed."

A man walks into a bar and sits down next to a lady and a dog.

The man asks, "Does your dog bite?".

The lady answers, "Never!"

The man reaches out to pet the dog and the dog bites him.

The man says, "I thought you said your dog doesn't bite!"

The woman replies, "He doesn't. This isn't my dog."

A man walks into a bar with a newt on his shoulder.

"Interesting," says the bartender. "What's its name?"

"Tiny."

The bartender smiles and shrugs. "Why do you call it Tiny?"

"Because it's my newt."

A guy is complaining to his bartender that he's being plagued by strange dreams.

"One night I dream I'm a teepee, the next night I dream I'm a wigwam—every night, either a teepee or a wigwam. It's really starting to get to me."

The bartender responds, "It's clear what your problem is. You're two tents!"

A man asks the only other guy in the bar if he can buy him a drink.

"Of course," comes the reply.

The first man then asks him, "Where are you from?"

"Ireland," replies the second.

"I'm from Ireland, too! Let's have another round, to Ireland."

"Cheers!" replies the other, and they both toss back their drinks.

The first man asks, "Where in Ireland are you from?"

"Dublin," comes the reply.

"I can't believe it!" says the first man. "I'm from Dublin, too! Let's have another drink, to Dublin!

Then the first man asks, "What school did you go to?"

"St. Mary's," replies the second. "I graduated in '65."

"This is unbelievable," the first man says. "I went to St. Mary's and graduated in '65, too!"

About this time another man sits down at the bar. "What's going on?" he asks the bartender.

"Not much," he replies. "The O'Sullivan twins are drunk again."

This guy walks into a bar, pulls out a gun, and says to the bartender, "Give me all your money or you're Geography!"

Surprised, the bartender says, "Surely, you mean History."

The robber replies, "Don't change the subject!"

FUTURE IMPERFECT

Humans have never been satisfied with the present. Against all logic, we demand to know the future, and we will use just about any object, natural or man-made, to pry it loose from the grip of mystery. "There is no nation, civilized or barbarian," said Cicero, "which does not believe that there are signs of the future and persons who interpret them."

Divination, it's called—or augury or soothsaying or haruspicy or foreknowledge or clairvoyance or prescience or vaticination or prophecy.

The synonyms extend to the far horizon, and whenever we encounter such a large bank of variant names for any given idea, we know that we are in the presence of intense preoccupation and a very long history.

Many of the nouns that designate these attempts to tell the future end in the letters -*mancy*. This combining form comes from the Greek word -*manteia,* meaning prophecy. (I'll bet you saw *that* one coming.) The hundreds of terms that use this word part offer us a mini-course in history, sociology, theology, psychology, and word formation. And, of course, like all specialized words, they're just plain fun.

People have long believed that the great outdoors is full of messages about the future. They studied the patterns of fallen flower petals (anthomancy), of fig leaves on a branch (botanomancy), and of laurel leaves (daphnomancy). Pebbles were predictors (psephomancy), as well as stones (lithomancy), and pearls had more than monetary value (margaritomancy). In addition, the direction of the wind (aeromancy), cloud formations (chaomancy), bubbles rising in a pool of water (pegomancy), patterns in the dust (amathomancy), digging things out of the ground (oryctomancy), the appearance of the heavens (uranomancy), meteors (meteoromancy), the phases of the moon (selenomancy), the alignment of the stars (astromancy), and the movement of tides (hydromancy) have all spoken to true believers. Could it be that amathomancy is the reason we often see the words *Wash me* scrawled on the dusty door of a car?

Talking and listening to the animals preceded Dr. Doolittle by thousands of years. Zoomancy observed the behavior of animals to foretell events, and theriomancy saw mystical meaning in the movements of wild beasts. Ornithomancy studied the beckoning flight of birds, ailuromancy paid attention to where jumping cats landed, icthyomancy studied the telltale entrails of fish, and hippomancy heard meaning in the nervous neighing of horses. The elegant scurrying of mice was significant in myomancy, and which grain of corn a rooster would choose was at the heart of alectryomancy. Ophiomancy focused on sibilant snakes, and spatulamancy depended on the burned and cracked shoulder blades of sacrificial sheep. Cephalanomancy saw practitioners boiling the head of an ass to study its skull. Alive or dead, there was no such thing as a dumb animal; they all spoke.

The human body could lean toward to the future, too. Checking the number of knots in an umbilical cord was omphalomancy. One's very appearance was significant (schematomancy), as was one's posture (ichnomancy). We hope that it wasn't overdrawn, but your blood was significant (hematomancy). Lines on the soles of your feet? Welcome to pedomancy. Lines on your forehead? Call it metopomancy. Wrinkled neck? Welcome to collimancy. Your fingernails were involved in onychomancy, and your teeth in odontomancy. Read my lips (labiomancy) was more than a campaign slogan, and people were watching your tongue even if you weren't (hyomancy). Even your stomach rumblings were listened to (gastromancy).

Evidently, centuries ago, mothers must not have made such a big fuss about their children playing with food. A nursing mother would see meaning in which breast her infant chose (mazomancy). Alphitomancy used barley meal to see into the future, tyromancy studied the coagulation patterns of cheese, and eggs weren't always what they were cracked up to be when engaged in oomancy — also called ovomancy. You needed figs for sycomancy, onions for cromnyomancy, flour for aleuromancy, and salt for halomancy. Drinkers could use wine for oenomancy, but to see the wave of the future, teetotalers had to make do with a basin (lecanomancy) or a bowl of water (kylixomancy).

Where there's smoke, there's fire — and a potential light on the future. Seers claimed to be able to interpret the patterns of burning coals (anthracomancy) or of ashes (spodomancy and cineromancy). They saw significant meaning in the ease or difficulty of blowing out ceremonial candles (pneumancy). A pit fire (pyromancy) or a lamp flame (lampadomancy and lychnomancy) could foreshadow things, and *Smoke Gets in Your Eyes* must have been the theme song of those who studied burning incense (libanomancy and knissomancy), smoke (capnomancy) ascending from a pyre, and burning straws (sideromancy).

Sharp objects pointed the way to the future during those days. Forficomancy used suspended shears, belomancy involved arrows with incised marks or words, axinomancy employed a hatchet balanced on a bar, you needed a sword for the art of machaeromancy, and indiscriminate aichmomancy was satisfied with any old pointed object at all.

At times, ancient futurology must have resembled modern Las Vegas. Dice were employed in astragalomancy, cleromancy, and cubomancy, and someone had to deal the cards in cartomancy (also called chartomancy). Today's carnival aficionados would have appreciated cheiromancy (palm reading) and spheromancy (crystal gazing). The latter two were also called chiromancy and crystallomancy.

Of course, dealing with the future wasn't always an academic exercise; it could sometimes get very messy. Consider studying human entrails (anthropomancy and splanchnomancy), feces (scatomancy, spatilomancy, and stercomancy), or urine (ouromancy, urimancy, urinomancy, and uromancy). "Waste not, want not," must have been the prime directive in those days.

To its credit, the prediction industry seems to have been an equal opportunity employer. The gamut ran from gods and angels (theomancy and angelomancy) to demons and evil spirits (demonomancy and necyomancy). Laughter could send a message (gelomancy), but so could tears (dacryomancy).

The smallest object nearby told a tale (micromancy), but so did the largest object nearby (macromancy). From top of the head (cephalomancy) to sole of the foot (pedomancy), and from embryo (amniomancy) to wrinkled old neck (collimancy), the universe and all that dwelt therein waxed eloquent.

Wax? Oh, yes: that was ceromancy.

NAMES THAT FIT
LIKE A GLOVE

What's in a name? That which we call a rose
By any other word would smell as sweet.
Romeo & Juliet, II.ii. 1-2

Well, that's literally true, Bill, but I think a little of the bloom would be taken off if we called a rose a skunk, let's say, or vomit. Names do carry connotations as part of their baggage. It's true even of our family names. How would you like to be Nicholas Nerd or Lucinda Schitz?

There's an interesting class of names that some people tend to treat far too seriously, which is evident from the academic name: nominative determinism. This is the theory that some people unconsciously choose their occupations in life because of their name. Obviously, a large number of surnames arose historically because of the work that family founders did: Archer, Baker, Butcher, Carpenter, Fletcher (arrow maker), Fuller (cloth cleaner), Miller, Shepherd, and Smith. But that doesn't mean that subsequent generations were doomed to ply that occupation. Detective Lew Archer carried a gun, not a bow. I never saw a picture of Alan Shepard carrying sheep into space, and Henry Miller didn't always have his nose to the grindstone.

But the humorous element of names that match one's occupation is what attracts most people. Franklin P. Adams coined the term aptronym to designate a name that is suited to a profession. And so we have Roy Holler, auctioneer; James Bugg, exterminator; Linda Toot, flautist; Dorothy Reading, librarian; Marvin Dime, coin dealer; and Priscilla Flattery, publicist. Let's take a look at some categories that have more than their share of suitable names.

CLERGY

- Rev. James R. God is minister of the Baptist Church in Congress, South Carolina
- Father Papa is assigned to St. Agnes Church in West Chester, PA.
- Rev. D. Goodenough is a Methodist minister
- Donald Goodness is the rector of the Church of the Ascension in New York City
- There is a feminist theologian named Dr. Carol Christ. It is not known if she is related to Father Raymond Christ of the Archdiocese of Philadelphia.
- The Rev. Samuel Abbot is an Episcopalian priest, as is Rev. George Easter. Father Donald Abbot serves the Catholic Diocese of Charleston.
- Fathers Grim and Gross belong to the Catholic Diocese of Fargo.

DENTISTS

- Dr. Tom Fillar is a dentist.
- So are Dr. Aichen and Dr. Chiew.
- Dr. Hertz was a dentist in Ft. Lauderdale.
- Doctors Akamine and Auh practice in Los Angeles.
- Dr. Yankelovich is a dentist in Palos Heights, Illinois.
- Dr. Les Plack is a dentist in the San Francisco Bay Area.

DOCTORS

- Dr. Dick Chopp is an Austin, Texas, vasectomy specialist; his associate is Dr Hardman.
- Joseph C. Babey is a pediatrician.
- Dr. Harry Beaver is a Virginia gynecologist.
- American Urological Association members include Dr. P.P. Peters, Dr. Wiener, Dr. Cox, Dr. Dick, and Dr. John Thomas.
- Dr. Fingers is a gynecologist in Australia.
- Dr. Dick Bone is an osteopath.
- Marcellene Doctor is a dermatologist in Fall River, Massachusetts.
- A physician in Maine is named Dr. DeKay.
- Michele Hakakha is a Beverly Hills gynecologist, and Leland

Lapp and Elden Pecka deliver in San Diego.
- Dr. I. Doctor is an opthalmologist.
- Drs. Kent Aftergut, Harold Lancer, and Kenneth Mark remove tattoos.
- Bracebridge, Ontario, Canada, is home to an optometrist named Gord Looker.
- Dr. Frank Noodleman helps restore hair.
- Sir Russell Brain is a famous English neurologist.
- Dr. Peter Bump is a gynecologist in Traverse City, Michigan.
- Dr. Slaughter is an oral surgeon.
- Urologist Dr. Dick Tapper has a practice near Buffalo.
- There is a chiropractor in Tacoma, Washington, named Dr. Bonz.
- Dr. Nurse is a General Practitioner at the Woodlawn Medical Centre, Dartmouth, Nova Scotia.
- Dr. Treadwell is the head of the pediatric orthopedic department of Vancouver General Hospital.
- Drs. Joel Cook, Alexander Gross, and Anne Lott are dermatologic surgeons specializing in fat transfer.
- Both Dr. C.B. Footlick and Dr. Smelsey were podiatrists.

LAWYERS

- In Traverse City, Michigan, three lawyers are named Justice, Robb, and Law.
- The Florida Bar directory lists lawyers named Law, Justice, Just, Juster, and Judge.
- If your reputation has been defiled, you may want to consult with Boston's Joshua Stayn, and if you pay by the hour, Florida's Kathy Klock might be your pick.
- Michael Ram will help you with Military Law, but not as avidly as Michael Guerra (Spanish for war).
- Claudia T. Salomon specializes in Dispute Resolution.
- Linda Pence of Indianapolis will be happy to help you with Gaming Law.
- Daniel Saylor specializes in Maritime Law.
- In Rochester, David Tennant will help you with Real Estate Law.
- For help with Hazardous Waste laws, turn to Wayne

Greenfeder or Frank Hunger.
- California's Steven Richman specializes in Banking and Finance Law.
- Florida's Allison Folds handles divorce cases.
- If you're having trouble with an online store, New York's Kenneth Payment is a specialist in Internet Law.
- In Hammond, Indiana, Paul Rake specializes in Environmental Law.
- The Western part of Ireland is home to the firm of Argue and Phibbs.
- In Coral Gables, Gail Parenti handles nursing home cases; in Seattle, it's Claudia Kilbreath.

RESEARCHERS/PROFESSORS

- Richard Seed is a pioneer of reproductive technology.
- A paper on incontinence in the *British Journal of Urology* was authored by J.W. Splatt and D. Weedon.
- Prof. Martin Braine is an American cognitive psychologist.
- S.M. Breedlove writes on sexual dimorphism for the *Journal of Neuroscience.*
- Gene Shearer is a Biologist with the U.S. National Institute of Health.
- The American expert on deformed frogs is Professor Hoppe of Southwest University of Minnesota.
- Professor Michael Lean is the Professor of Nutrition at the University of Glasgow.
- Edgar E. Mountain wrote "Geology of Southern Africa".
- Dr. Randolph Seed worked on a project on artificial insemination at the Reproduction and Fertility Clinic in Chicago.
- M. Bedrock wrote a thesis on "Sedimentology of some Westphalian C sequences".
- "How fish hear and make sounds at the same time" was an article by Andrew Bass.
- Dr. Reginald A. Beach specializes in coastal dynamics and sediment transport in the surf zone.
- Dr. David Bird, of McGill University in Montréal, is one of the best known Canadian ornithologists.
- Dr. Henry Head is past editor of *Brain,* a medical journal.

- Professor William F. Dolphin of Boston University is a researcher in marine mammal sonar.
- Steven Haddock is a scientist at the Monterey Bay Aquarium Research Institute.
- Peter Herring works at the Southampton Oceanography Centre in England.
- Dr. Sam Lake is a freshwater ecologist in the Department of Biological Sciences at Monash University.
- Dr. James Makepeace, professor of sociology at the college of St. Benedict at St. John's University in Minnesota, was a specialist in family violence.
- An article entitled "Cognitive Rehabilitation of Amnesiac Alcoholics" was written by B.J. Spittle.
- Sally Marine was an administrator at the Southampton Oceanography Centre.
- Peter Cliff writes about mountain navigation.

PSYCHIATRISTS

- Specialists in Child and Adolescent Psychiatry include Doctors Alters, Better, Best, Brain, Childs, Denton, Gabby, Goodfriend, Gross, Hack, Handler, Hugg, Joy, Klam, Krier, Kuhl, Kuts, Lapp, Lineback, Little, Luckie, Ma, Martini, Mee, Miner, Mullarky, Muse, Mutter, Narcisi, Noel, Noh, Nutter, Pagan, Panik, Pastor, Patt, Pine, Rahtz, Render, Riddle, Root, Ruberman, Sack, Sane, Schield, Schmek, Schramm, Shampain, Shnaps, Shopper, Skuse, Slack, Small, Smoke, Snow, Sorter, Spar, Speck, Spitz, Stage, Stark, Storm, Stuck, Sugar, Surpris, Tan, Tarr, Termini, Tingle, Trott, Tweed, Valentine, Van der Gaag, Vary, Walkup, Ward, Wild, Wind, Wing, Wolf, Work, Wruble, Wurst, and Young.
- Drs. John Kluck, Richard Worst, and Charles Covert are forensic psychiatrists.

SPORTS

- Robert Furlong, racing commissioner.
- Matt Batts, baseball player who started with Boston in 1947. Inappropriately, his record was similar to that of Clyde Kluttz

of the St. Louis Cardinals.
- Speaking of baseball, we can't forget the Tiger's Cecil Fielder.
- Lake Speed, race car driver, who handed in the keys after nineteen years on the circuit.
- Gary Player, golfer from South Africa.
- Rollie Fingers pitched for the Oakland A's.
- Dale Kickett played for the Freemantle Football Club.
- Nathan Leeper, high jumper in the 2000 Sydney Olympics.
- Dick Trickle, NASCAR driver.
- Olympic swimmers have included Bottom (1980), Crabbe (1928), Float (1984), Goessling (1908), Spitz (1972), and Watters (1988).
- In Newcastle, Australia, there is a boxer named Darren Hitwell.
- Margaret Court and Anna Smashnova were tennis players

VETERINARIANS

- In Baton Rouge, there is a veterinarian named Dr. Daniel Beaver.
- Dr. Mike Bassett practices veterinary medicine.
- Dr. Daniel Bone specializes in animal orthopedics.
- Dr. James Chase specializes in equine medicine.
- A veterinarian in Bogart, Georgia, is named Dr. Crowe.
- Dr. William Hay treats horses.
- Boston is home to veterinarian Nicholas Trout.
- One of Dr. Woodies' research interests (Lexington, KY) is Equine Urogenital.

Whether there are subtle psychological underpinnings to this phenomenon or whether it is sheer coincidence, keep your notebook handy the next time you receive a service. Your stockbroker may be Risky, your grocer may be Cabbage, and the policeman that stops you for speeding may be Badger.

DUM & DUMMER

There is no sin except stupidity. — Oscar Wilde

Our parents taught us not to speak negatively of others, but what's a person to do when ignorance, the absence of knowledge, rears its empty head? Any thesaurus will provide us with substantives such as blockheadedness, denseness, doltishness, dumbness, dullness, stupidity, shallowness, incomprehension, unintelligence, and unenlightenment, but when we need heftier words or more striking language, where do we turn?

There is, of course, the stinging power of simile and metaphor, though I fear that the frequent impulse to chastise dolts in picturesque language inevitably leads to clichés. Among others, we have the following at our disposal:

- dumb bunny,
- dumb as an ox,
- dodo
- dumb as a slug
- harebrain
- dumb as a Junebug
- dumb as a carp
- dumb as a dead moose
- dumb as a jackass
- birdbrain
- featherbrain

We are not very respectful of our finned, furred, and feathered friends, but inanimate objects take a beating, too — particularly, for some unaccountable reason, when they are in containers. Thus, we have

- dumb as a sack of doorknobs
- dumb as a bag of nails
- dumb as a sack of hammers
- dumb as a box of dirt
- dumb as a box of rocks
- dumb as a box of hair
- dumb as a sack of excrement — presumably left over from the previous list.

Then there are the loose objects, such as

- dumb as a brick
- dumb as a post
- dumb as a tree stump
- dumb as a doorstop
- dumb as a stop sign
- dumb as a doornail
- dumb as a mud fence
- dumb as a stick
- dumb as a wooden bucket
- dumb as a pair of cleats
- dumb as a divot
- dumb as a wedge
- dumb as a 2x4
- dumb as a mudflap
- dumb as a lampshade
- dumb as a stale chunk of meatloaf
- dumb as a wall
- dumb as a shoelace
- dumb as a diaper
- dumb as a rope
- dumb as a ball of clay

Why am I suddenly reminded of a garage sale?

We can see the dangers of triteness here, especially when fending off infinite imbecility. So I offer the following primer of useful terms to describe industrial-strength stupidity.

asininity
Utter stupidity or silliness [L. *asinus,* ass]
"Meek, even to a degree of asininity, in his demeanor." John
Kennedy, *Annals of Quodlibet*

benightedness
The dark night of the mind [be-, *completely,* + night]
"Respectable old Russell Whigs, on whom charges of moral
corruption operate much more powerfully than charges of
intellectual benightedness." *The Pall Mall Gazette*
Another form of this rather gentle putdown is benightment:
"The benightment of superstition." Archibald Alison, *History
of Europe*

bêtise
Folly; stupidity; ignorance [Fr. *bête,* beast, foolish]
"... one more exhibition of the bêtise of an audience when
confronted with something fresh." Arnold Bennett

Boeotian
Dull; stupid [from the ancient district of Boeotia in east central
Greece, noted for its moist, thick atmosphere, which allegedly
dulled the senses]
"The heavy atmosphere of that Boeotia might be good for
vegetation, but it was associated in popular belief with the
dullness of the Boeotian intellect." John Cardinal Newman,
The Idea of a University

crassitude
Gross ignorance or stupidity [L. *crassus,* solid or dense]
"Amy, not being afflicted with crassitude, soon did her work
admirably." Mortimer Collins, *Marquis & Merchant*

doltishness
Stupidity [O.E. *dol,* inert of intellect]
"The usual doltishness of the regal race." SHELLEY in Dowden
Life

duncery
Intellectual Dullness [<Duns Scotus]
"The more of duncery they have, the more of pride, and the greater is their ambition." Erasmus, *On Folly*

fatuity
Foolish stupidity [L. *fatuus*, foolish]
"O strange fatuity of youth!" William Makepeace Thackeray, *The Virginians*

ignoramus
An ignorant person [L. *ignoramus*, we do not know]
"So ignorant am I and by such ignoramuses surrounded." William Cowper, *private correspondence*

ignoration
Complete or utter ignorance [L. *ignorare*, not to know]
"... the ignoration of the true relation of each organism to its environment." Alfred North Whitehead

inerudition
Ignorance; unlearned condition [L. *in*, not + *erudire*, to instruct]
"I ... being too conscious of my own inerudition to be able to instruct others." Charles Cotton, tr. *Montaigne*

inscience
Want of knowledge; ignorance [L. *in*, not + *scientia*, knowledge]
"His special pleading is matched by his inscience of every technical law term." Benson, *Cyprian*

insulsity
Stupidity; senselessness [L. *in*, not + *salsus*, witty]
"To justify the counsels of God and Fate from the insulsity of mortal tongues." John Milton, *The Doctrine and Discipline of Divorce*

mopishness
Foolishness; stupidity [<*mope*, to be in a stupefied state]
"By degrees she fell into a perfect mopishness or stupidity."
Sloane *Voy. Islands*

moria
Mental dullness or retardation [Gr. *moros*, foolish]
"Moria, thus explained, will be found, as a genus, to embrace the two following species: 1. Moria imbecillis. Imbecility. 2.demens. Irrationality." S. Cooper, *Good's Study Med.* (ed. 3)

moronism
Ignorance; imbecility [Gr. *moros*, foolish]
"Willful obfuscation in a writer is completely indefensible... It is the ugly matching bookend of that other moronism, the greeting card verse." *Los Angeles Times Book Review*

nescience
Lack of knowledge; ignorance [L. *ne*, not + *scire*, to know]
"His apparent nescience of contemporary literature was not a pose." Arthur Quiller-Couch

nincompoopery
Foolishness; stupidity [origin uncertain]
"What is so apparent is that gullibility and nincompoopery overtake critical common sense and all safeguards are abandoned in the face of guile, deception, and self-deception." *Skeptical Inquirer*

nitwittery
Imbecility [prob. Icelandic *nit*, louse egg + wit]
"The two houses, of course, were the...feuding families of Romeo and Juliet, whose nitwit hatred would indirectly cause Mercutio's departure for Paradise." K. Vonnegut *Hocus Pocus*

obtuseness
Lack of intelligence [L. *obtusus*, dulled]
"Nor did this arise from any insensibility or obtuseness of his intellectual parts." Laurence Sterne, *Tristram Shandy*

ostrichism
The deliberate avoidance or ignorance of conditions as they exist
"Ostrichism will not, of course, save one single American."
Pearl Buck

rusticity
A lack of intellectual culture; ignorance [L. *rus,* country]
"He began laughing at my rusticity." Benjamin Malkin,
Adventures of Gil Blas

sciolism
Pretentious superficiality of knowledge [L. *sciolus,* smatterer]
"That epidemic of a proud ignorance occasioned by a diffused
sciolism." Coleridge, *The Statesman's Manual*

sottage
Foolishness; stupidity [O.F. *sot,* fool]
"Hard Iron-Ages, death-declining sottage." C. Fitzgeffrey *Sir
F. Drake*

stultification
 Foolish ignorance [L. *stultus,* foolish]
"The dullards become more stultified than ever." C. H.
Grandgent

stupiditarian
One whose ruling principle is stupidity [L. *stupere,*
benumbed]
A heavy-headed stupiditarian in official station, veiling the
sheerest incompetency in a mysterious sublimity of carriage!"
WHIPPLE *Lit. & Life*

ultracrepidation
The action or fact of criticizing ignorantly [L. phrase *ultra
crepidam,* beyond the sole] "It is always dangerous, as Coleridge
phrased it, to ultracrepidate." Frederic W. Farrar

vacuity
Complete absence of ideas [L. *vacuus*, empty]
"Though more to folly than to guilt inclined, a drear vacuity possess'd my mind." Hannah More, *A Search After Happiness*

Use these terms intelligently, and your friends and neighbors may come to regard you as an agnoiologist — a person who engages in the metaphysical study of ignorance.

PARDON ME, MYTH

There are more myths floating around on the internet about the origin of words and phrases than there are fruit flies on a rotten banana. Most of them, quite obviously, are the invention of imaginative jokesters—probably English teachers on summer vacation—who enjoy gulling the gullible. I'll grant that these stories often show imagination and verve, but when they are taken as gospel and inserted in cascading e-mails which clog the inbox and the brain, it's time to call a halt.

In this chapter, I'm going to cover some of the phony stories that I've encountered. Some are silly, some are funny, and some have the ring of possibility, but all of them are provably wrong. They do illustrate a common human tendency: when we don't know the origin of something, we become uneasy. Humans are fabricators; we would rather make something up or grasp at an off-the-wall explanation than admit that no one knows—admit that some things simply have been lost in the mists of history.

Above board (in full view; honestly)
MYTH: The board was the deck of a ship. When you approached a vessel, if the crew was inexplicably out of sight (below board) you were prudent to suspect pirates.
REALITY: A board was a table, and when card-playing gamblers slipped their hands under the table, or board, cheating was assumed.

Amazon   (in Greek mythology, a nation of women warriors)

MYTH: They took their name from the Greek word *a-mazos*, without a breast. This is because they voluntarily cut off their right breasts to be able to use a bow and arrow to maximum effect.

REALITY: The Greeks borrowed the term from the Iranian *ha-mazon*, "fighting together."

Big wig (a very important person)

MYTH: Wealthy men could afford good wigs made from wool. The wigs couldn't be washed, so to clean them they would carve out a loaf of bread, put the wig in the shell, and bake it for 30 minutes. The heat would make the wig big and fluffy; hence, the term big wig.

REALITY: It's hard to imagine a more ludicrous cleaning method. Baking a loaf of bread a second time would result in a hard chunk of toast. Instead of making the wig fluffy, it would constrict it, thus creating a really bad hair day. However, the term *big wig* did originate with the large and ornate wigs that only the wealthy could afford.

Chairman   (the presiding officer of an assembly, meeting, committee, or board)

MYTH: In the late 1700s, many houses consisted of a large room with only one chair. The head of the household always sat in the chair while everyone else ate sitting on the floor. To sit in the chair meant you were important and made you the "chairman."

REALITY: Obviously, these people never took an art history course. By that era, everyone had chairs or benches, as painting after painting will testify. The chairman was the person who sat in the chair of authority at the head of the table in a political or business situation; it had nothing to do with daddy scarfing down dinner.

Chew the fat   (to spend time chatting)

MYTH: People in the Middle Ages would hang a side of smoked bacon near their open fireplace to show that they were prosperous. When a guest came, they would slice off a strip, and the host and the guest would sit there contentedly, chewing the fat.

REALITY: In its current sense, this phrase didn't even exist until the late 19th century. No one is absolutely sure where it came from, but it may originally have meant constant complaining, not just idle conversation. It should be treated as an analogy: just as the jaws grind away relentlessly when chewing gristly meat, so move the jaws of the inveterate talker.

Cold enough to freeze the balls off a brass monkey (really, really cold!)

MYTH: On sailing ships, cannon balls were stacked in pyramid shape using a triangular piece of brass called the monkey. When it got cold enough, the metal would contract, and the cannon balls would scatter all over the deck.

REALITY: There is no historical evidence validating "monkey" in this sense. In fact, cannon balls were stored below deck near the cannons on <u>wooden</u> racks with holes in them (shot racks or shot garlands). Rolling cannon balls would have been totally unacceptable, a toe-crunching danger to the crew on a rocking vessel. Like it or not, what we have here is a vulgar anatomical reference. Herman Melville had a character say this in his seafaring novel *Omoo*: "It was 'ot enough to melt the nose h'off a brass monkey." The temperatures are opposite and the body parts differ, but the affinity is obvious.

Cold shoulder (deliberate disregard or disrespect)

MYTH: In the Middle Ages [*here we go again!*], unwelcome guests were given a cold shoulder of meat rather than the customary hot meal. They would get the message that they were unwanted, and be on their way the next day.

REALITY: Meat of any kind was a luxury in the Middle Ages, not a thinly coded message. The phrase doesn't even show up in print until 1816, when Sir Walter Scott used it in *The Antiquary*. Its use in that novel makes it clear that it referred to human anatomy, not mutton. It's a dismissive shrug, a prelude to turning one's back on someone.

Cop (police officer)

MYTH: This is an acronym for "Constable on Patrol" or "Constabulary of Police" or . . . [fill in the blank.] Alternatively, it started because policemen wore copper buttons on their uniforms.

REALITY: It arose because of what they did: capture people. As a verb, cop was a slang term for "grab" in Great Britain in the late 18th/early 19th century. Ultimately, it tracks back to the Latin verb *capere*, to take or seize.

Cost an arm and a leg (heavy price to pay)

MYTH: In George Washington's day, there were no cameras. One's image was either sculpted or painted. Some paintings of George Washington showed him standing behind a desk with one arm behind his back while others showed both legs and both arms. Prices charged by painters were not based on how many people were to be painted, but by how many limbs were to be painted. Arms and legs are limbs; therefore, painting them would cost the buyer more. Hence the expression "Okay, but it'll cost you an arm and a leg."

REALITY: It has nothing to do with physical reality. It's a deliberate hyperbole, an exaggerated statement, much like "This'll kill you!" "That blew me away!" "I work my fingers to the bone," and "I split my sides laughing!" Besides, it doesn't appear until the 20th century.

Crack a smile (produce the beginnings of a smile)

MYTH: In the old days, many women and men had developed acne scars by adulthood. The women would spread bee's wax over their facial skin to smooth out their complexions. If a woman smiled, the wax would crack, leading to the expression, "to crack a smile."

REALITY: First, refer to **mind your own beeswax**. Second, to crack a smile literally means to part the lips slightly, the same way we'd say, "crack that window open a bit," or "leave that door open a crack."

Devil to pay (serious trouble is foreseen)

MYTH: The devil is the long seam at the ship's keel, and *paying* meant caulking that seam with tar, a very dirty and difficult job.

REALITY: This one is marginal. Originally, it was a reference to paying the devil with your eternal soul, the core of the Faust legend presented by Christopher Marlowe, Johann Wolfgang von Goethe, and countless imitators. It first shows up in print in Jonathon Swift's *Journal to Stella*, and there it is a reference to the ultimate payment: eternal damnation. At a much later date, sailors may have latched on to it because of the meaning overlap, but that wasn't the source; that was an adaptation.

Frog in one's throat   (hoarseness or phlegm in the throat)

MYTH: it was a common practice in the Middle Ages to stick a frog in a patient's mouth when he or she had a throat infection known as thrush.

REALITY: Just think about that alleged treatment: do you think that people would let some clown shove a frog down their throats when they could hardly breathe already? *A frog in my throat* refers to a temporary thickness in the voice, especially of a radio talk show host. It's an allusion to the hoarse, throaty croaking of frogs.

Golf   (a game which Mark Twain described as "a good walk spoiled")

MYTH: Golf is an old acronym for <u>G</u>entlemen <u>O</u>nly, <u>L</u>adies <u>F</u>orbidden.

REALITY: No one knows for sure, but there is some speculation that it may come from the Dutch word *kolf,* a club or bat. At any rate, it wasn't a sexist slogan. Besides, before the 20th century, acronyms were nonexistent.

Gossip   (rumor or talk of a personal, sensational, or intimate nature)

MYTH: Early politicians required feedback from the public, so they sent their assistants to local pubs to "go sip some ale" and listen to people's conversations and political concerns. "Go sip" soon turned into the word gossip.

REALITY: The word comes from the Anglo-Saxon *godsibb,* a godparent or spiritual relative. By the Middle Ages, the word had come to mean a close friend. The modern use of the word to mean idle (often spiteful) conversation was in place by the 19th century

hunky-dory   (perfectly satisfactory; fine)

MYTH: American sailors docking in Yokohama Japan would head for the red light district on a street named Huncho-Dori.

REALITY: A very popular song sung by the original Christy Minstrels during the Civil War (*Josephus Orange Blossom*) contained the line, "red-hot hunky-dory contraband." This slang term meant "in good condition," and it probably evolved from a Dutch word *honk*, meaning "home" or "goal" as in a game of tag. Once you reached *honk*, everything was hunky-dory.

Keep your nose to the grindstone (keep on working assiduously)

MYTH: This is a reference to the old water-powered grist mill and its huge grinding stone. The miller had to check adjustments by sniffing. If the stone was set too close to the grain, the meal would overheat and begin to burn. His nose would alert him.

REALITY: The grindstone was the sharpening tool used by a blacksmith. Originally, the phrase indicated harshness or implacable cruelty that could wear a person down.

Let the cat out of the bag (disclose the real truth)

MYTH: The cat was the cat-o-nine-tails, the whip used to punish wayward sailors aboard sailing vessels. It was kept in a sealed bag to protect it from the elements. When it was taken out of the bag, the terrible truth was revealed: you are about to be flogged.

REALITY: It is probably a reference to a scam that was perpetrated on rural folk visiting cathedral towns and their markets in the Middle Ages. A slaughtered suckling pig was displayed to the buyer. If a price was agreed upon, the seller would pull a bait-and-switch by putting a shaved dead cat into a sack out of view of the buyer. The weight and the feel through the sacking would fool the victim until he got home. There, he would take the cat out of the bag and discover to his chagrin that he had been duped. This phrase is mirrored by "to buy a pig in a poke" (a sack).

Losing face (to suffer embarrassment; to be publicly humiliated)

MYTH: In the old days, many women and men had developed acne scars by adulthood. The women would spread bee's wax over their facial skin to smooth out their complexions. When they sat too close to the fire, the wax would melt, leading to the expression "losing face."

REALITY: See **mind your own beeswax**. First of all, if your face was covered with wax, body heat alone would be enough to soften it. Second, there is no doubt that the term arose only in the late nineteenth century, and that it is a translation of the Chinese *tiu lien*. The opposite is to save face. How would they explain that? Women sat on a block of ice to save face?

Mind your own beeswax (stay out of my business)

MYTH: In the old days, many women and men had developed acne scars by adulthood. The women would spread bee's wax over their facial skin to smooth out their complexions. When they were speaking to each other, if a woman began to stare at another woman's face she was told "mind your own bee's wax."

REALITY: It never happened. The term developed in the 1930s as a humorous variant on the word *business*.

News (information reported by the media)

MYTH: Since reports come from all parts of the compass (North, East, West, and South), the acronym NEWS was invented.

REALITY: Plain and simple, it refers to new information. In fact, when it showed up in English in the 14th century, a translation of the French *noveles*, it was spelled *newes*, which ruins the so-called acronym. Remember: no acronyms before 1900.

Not enough room to swing a cat (cramped quarters)

MYTH: The cat was the cat-o-nine-tails, the whip used to punish wayward sailors aboard sailing vessels. To effect the punishment, the quartermaster had to have enough room to swing the whip freely. Otherwise, the punishment would be far too lenient.

REALITY: Spare me! Go back and read **Let the cat out of the bag**. This is one for PETA to deal with. We're talking about cruelty to animals here.

Not playing with a full deck (below normal intelligence)

MYTH: A tax was levied when purchasing playing cards, but it applied only to the Ace of Spades. To avoid paying the tax, people would purchase the other 51 cards instead. Since most games require 52 cards, these people were thought to be stupid or dumb because they weren't "playing with a full deck."

REALITY: There was a tax on playing cards, but the tax stamp was used to seal the entire box, not just one card. This phrase joins a host of other picturesque ways of saying dumb, and none is meant literally: not the sharpest knife in the drawer, a few sandwiches short of a picnic, his wheel is turning but the hamster is dead, etc.

Not worth a tinker's damn   (totally without value)

MYTH: In Scotland and Ireland, a tinker was an itinerant mender of household utensils. To solder a hole in a metal plate or pot, he would form a raised barrier of bread dough around the hole (a dam) to keep the solder from flowing where it wasn't needed. When the job was complete, he would remove the dough and throw it away.

REALITY: Tinkers were generally a scurrilous lot without roots who swore without cessation. So many curse words flowed from their mouths that they were totally devalued; any shock value was lost. In the early part of the 19th century, it was "tinker's damn." The Victorians later tried to clean it up by turning it into "tinker's dam."

Posh   (luxurious; suitable for the affluent)

MYTH: This phrase comes from ship travel between Britain and India on the fleet operated by the Peninsular and Oriental Steamship Company. P.O.S.H. is an acronym for Port Out, Starboard Home. A person with a cabin on the port side on the leg to India and a cabin on the starboard side returning to England had the best of everything: a cooling sea breeze and shelter from the unrelenting sun. Such accommodations were saved for wealthy frequent travelers, and their tickets were stamped with a P.O.S.H. designation.

REALITY: The highly specific nature of that explanation is what torpedoes it. The Peninsular and Oriental Steamship Company absolutely denies the story; there were no such tickets. The most likely origin is London street slang, where *posh* meant money. It is possible that it was adapted from Romany (the language of Gypsies), where *posh-houri* meant half-pence, and *posh-kooroona* meant half-crown.

Raining cats and dogs   (a driving, vicious rain)

MYTH: Houses in the Middle Ages had thatched roofs constructed of thick straw, piled high, with no wood underneath. They were the only place for the little animals to get warm. So all the pets—dogs, cats and other small animals, mice, rats, bugs—lived in the roof. When it rained, it became slippery, so sometimes the animals would slip and fall off the roof. Thus the saying, "it's raining cats and dogs."

REALITY: There's no question that bugs and mice and the occasional bird might live in a straw roof, but dogs and cats? Give me a break! And people in those days had wood-burning fireplaces to keep all creatures, great and small, warm. The explanation that I favor is that in 18th century London (not particularly noted for its urban hygiene), after a torrential downpour, gutters would overflow with garbage, sewage, and dead animals left by the side of the street, all of which would be swept along as if they had fallen with the rain. An alternative explanation is that in Norse mythology, cats and dogs were associated with Odin, the god of storms.

Rule of thumb (a useful principle, but one not strictly scientific or technical)

MYTH: In the old days, English common law allowed a man to discipline his wife by beating her, as long as the rod that he used was no thicker than a thumb.

REALITY: There was no such law on the books. Stupid men beat their wives occasionally, but it was not sanctioned by such a code. The saying refers to rough and ready measurement: the length of the first joint of a carpenter's thumb is about an inch long. *Rule* in this saying is a shortening for *ruler*. Likewise, a single pace covers about a foot, the distance from the tip of the nose to the outstretched fingers of an adult is roughly a yard, and horse heights are still measured by hands (the width of the palm and closed thumb is about four inches).

Saved by the bell (a last minute reprieve)

MYTH: In plague times, they often buried people alive because medical knowledge was limited. So they would tie a string on the "dead" person's wrist and thread it through a hole in the coffin and up through the ground and tie it to a bell. A watchman would have to sit out in the graveyard all night to listen for the bell. If the person were alive, he would be saved by the bell. He was a "dead ringer."

REALITY: Let's lay this one to rest. This isn't a case of the graveyard shift, the work shift that starts at midnight, which is a humorous reference to the hours when ghosts walk. This is a term from boxing. A pugilist who has been knocked down has until the count of 10 to get back up. If it's right at the end of a round and the end-of-round bell rings, the countdown stops. He is saved by the bell.

Shit (animal or human excrement)

MYTH: In the days of sailing ships [*a red light should go on*], manure was transported as fertilizer. It was stored at the very bottom of the boat to act as ballast, and when it got wet, it fermented and produced methane, an explosive gas. One little spark could ignite the gas and blow the ship to smithereens. So companies started marking the crates with the letters S.H.I.T. They stood for Ship High In Transit—don't put this where it will get wet.

REALITY: This is a very old word in English, and when it first appeared, it was not considered vulgar or indecent. In the year 1,000, for instance, it was used to refer to diarrhea in cattle. The Old English spelling for dung was *scite*, and it has its origin both in German and Dutch terms meaning the same thing.

Sincere (genuine; pure; true)

MYTH: In ancient Rome, unscrupulous sculptors would cover their mistakes and fill in any accidental holes with wax. It looked fine to the buyer, but a hot day would soon reveal the shoddy workmanship. Honest sculptors began to advertise their work as *sine cera*, Latin for "without wax."

REALITY: The actual origin is much more prosaic. The word *sincere* came into the English language around 1536 as a mirror of the Latin word *sincerus*, which meant pure, sound, and genuine.

Skins (a betting procedure in golf; winning a hole and its pot is "winning a skin")

MYTH: Fur trappers coming to Scotland from other countries, having spent months sailing in boats under primitive conditions would, instead of looking for female comfort, a bath, an alcoholic beverage, or a decent meal, opt for a round of golf before heading into town to sell their catch. As currency, they gambled their pelts or "skins" on golf, thus producing the term.

REALITY: No one has the definitive answer, but it's certainly not that one. One explanation says that *skins* derives from "skinning" an opponent. Golfers who lost a large amount of money were said to have been "skinned alive." The USGA says that *skins* (along with *cats* and *scats*) is a shortened version of *syndicates*. Finally, *The Oxford English Dictionary*, 2nd Edition, defines skin as American slang for a dollar.

Sleep tight (have a very satisfying and refreshing sleep)

MYTH: In medieval and colonial times, before modern box mattresses were invented, ropes were spread across the bed frame in a criss-cross pattern. The ropes would sag with use, so they had to be tightened periodically. If you didn't sleep tight, you had a sagging, uncomfortable mattress.

REALITY: "Tight" as an adverb meant *soundly*. To sleep tight was to sleep soundly. There were also references to a tight sleep—a sound sleep.

Snob (one who ignores social inferiors and plays up to social superiors)

MYTH: Undergraduates entering British universities were required to state whether they came from nobility or not. If not, their records were marked SNOB, which stood for the Latin phrase *sine nobilitate*, without nobility.

REALITY: It started out in the 18th century as a word designating a cobbler (shoemaker), a person of lower rank and status. Later, it was applied by collegians to a townie, as opposed to a gownie, so that probably helped stoke the myth.

Son of a gun (a scoundrel or rogue; sometimes even used affectionately)

MYTH: Boys who were born at sea under the protecting shelter of a cannon were given this name, as if the gun were the father.

REALITY: A single source entitled *Smyth's Sailor's Word-Book*, written in 1867—long after the fact—has led countless people astray.

He used the phrase, "cradled under the breast of a gun" to drive the story home. There are a few flaws in his claim. Daughters were born on board, too, but nowhere do we find "daughter of a gun." When the phrase first appeared in 1708, the context had nothing to do with the sea. Finally, it's a well-known euphemism used to replace the vulgar phrase *son of a bitch*. As happens with so many euphemisms, a rhyming word replaces the offensive term: son/gun. Aside from the 2nd edition of the *Oxford English Dictionary*, confirmation may be found in Suzanne Stark's *Female Tars: Women Aboard Ship in the Age of Sail* (Naval Institute Press, Annapolis Maryland):

"Births often took place on one of the tables between two guns on the lower deck, with only some canvas draped across to provide a modicum of privacy. From this situation comes the phrase 'son of a gun,' a euphemism for 'son of a bitch,' the assumption being that a child born between two guns on the lower deck was illegitimate, although in fact this was not usually the case."

Spud   (slang for potato)

MYTH: When the potato was introduced into Britain in the 16th century, it was viewed with great suspicion. The Powers That Be reasoned that it would be bad as a diet for ordinary people. Therefore, they formed the Society for the Prevention of an Unwholesome Diet (S.P.U.D.)

REALITY: Though human consumption of potatoes did get off to a slow start, there is no trace of any such society. Spud was the name for the tool used to dig a potato out of the ground, sort of a sharp spade. By the 19th century, it was applied to the vegetable itself. [General rule of thumb: acronyms began to be used only in the 20th century.]

Throw the baby out with the bath water   (discard the good along with the bad)

MYTH: In the Middle Ages, people took their yearly bath in May, but it was in a big communal tub that they would fill with hot water. The man of the house would get the privilege of the nice clean water. Then came all the other sons and men, then the women, and finally the children. Last came the babies. By then, the water was pretty thick. It was so dirty, you could literally lose someone in it.

REALITY: Can you imagine a mother *that* inattentive? This was always a figure of speech, not a literal reality. Originally, it was a German proverb from 1512: *das Kind mit den Bade ausschütten*. Three hundred years later (*not* the Middle Ages), it finally entered the English language when Thomas Carlyle translated it to make a point.

Tip (a gratuity given to reward good service)
MYTH: TIP is an acronym standing for <u>T</u>o <u>I</u>nsure <u>P</u>romptness.
REALITY: *Tip* was a 17th century underground slang term meaning "to pass on a small amount of money." By the 18th century, the verb had acquired the present meaning of a gratuity. There is a connection to the kind of surreptitious tip that one might receive about a particular horse race.

Turn the tables (reverse your relationship with someone to your own advantage)
MYTH: In Britain in the older days, removable table tops were finished on one side only in order to save money. When a family was alone, they used the unfinished side to avoid damage. When guests came to dinner, the good side was turned up.
REALITY: It may have come from the custom of reversing the table or board in games like checkers or backgammon so that opponents' positions are reversed. I have seen this happen in a version of Scrabble: at a predetermined time, players trade the tiles on their rack, making it a brand new challenge. After all, turnabout is fair play.

Wallop (to beat someone mercilessly)
MYTH: Henry VIII sent Sir John Wallop to carry out a reprisal raid on the French. In the course of his attack, he burned almost two dozen villages.
REALITY: There was such a man, but King Henry used him as a diplomat, not an avenging hammer. "Wallop" in the current sense didn't appear until 1823. It seems to have been imitative of the sound of a slap or blow. Before 1375 it meant to gallop.

Do me a favor, please. If you receive one or more of these myths in an e-mail, do NOT hit the forward button. You have a patriotic duty to free the ether of these verbal vampires. For heaven's sake, pound a stake into their insincere little hearts and put them to rest.

In the next chapter, we'll take a look at one of the most puzzling phrases ever devised.

TWENTY-SEVEN FEET OF MEASURED CONFUSION

The human mind is constructed in such a way that it leaps into action when it encounters something incomplete. It pulses and throbs and weaves until it has constructed a scenario from a whisper, a shadow, a blip of light, a hint of movement. It connects dots that are pure figments of the imagination Stark reality insists that some things will never be known or understood, but our inventive lobes quiver in electrochemical indignation at the very idea.

This has been driven home recently because of a subject which came up on my weekly radio program in Traverse City, Michigan. A caller asked the deceptively simple question, "Where did the phrase the whole nine yards (meaning "everything") come from?" I thought I knew, but I prudently said that I would do some research. Thank God (and Liberty Records) for Patience and Prudence, because the answer turns out to be elaborately confusing and inventively entertaining.

Before I list some of the explanations that have been circulating, let me quickly review a few of the principles that must guide anyone seeking to track down the original source of a word or phrase.

•Secondary sources just won't do. The fact that your beloved grandparent or knowledgeable neighbor assured you that something is true simply isn't good enough. If a phrase existed in the Middle Ages, then you must produce a primary source from that era, not from a book written centuries later.

•Even with a primary source, you must analyze the contemporary writer as thoroughly as possible. Did the writer invent the phrase, or is it a report? Is the writer reliable—that is, composing in a serious vein and in a field that he or she understands? Are there ulterior motives that would explain the writer's point of view?

•Is there independent confirmation in other reliable sources? Remember, speculative anachronism is a cottage industry in folk etymology. (Have you received the email entitled Life in the Middle Ages yet?)

•Is the explanation logical, consistent, plausible, and relevant, not just colorful? The fact that my television mast is nine yards long, though true, has nothing to do with this subject.

With that out of the way, here is what we know. The earliest known printed reference to the whole nine yards occurs in 1967 in Elaine Shepard's The Doom Pussy, a slightly fictionalized report about the Vietnam War published by Trident Press. The relevant section reads: "The story began when he had absent-mindedly gone through a wedding ceremony a couple of years before while snockered one Saturday night in San Francisco. Slipping out of the knot was expensive but Smash was eventually to untangle what he called 'the whole nine yards'." That's it. Nothing from ancient history, World Wars I or II, or The Journal of Sewing. Whether Ms. Shepard invented the phrase or was simply passing it on isn't known for certain. If she was a conduit, the phrase probably originated in the mid-1960s. Had it been significantly earlier, it would have appeared in an earlier printed source.

As Michael Quinion says in his World Wide Words web site, "If you're hoping for a definitive answer, you'd better buy a crystal ball. I have to say straight away this is one of the great unsolved mysteries of modern etymology, for which many seek the truth and almost as many find explanations, but hardly anyone has a clue."

Obviously, that doesn't stop people from pontificating. In fact, one of the surprising things I encountered is the passion with which people defend their version of the source for this elusive phrase. Why, they go the whole nine yards and then some!

Some of these pseudo-definitive explanations seem to be cut out of whole cloth. They claim that nine yards is

- the size of a nun's habit
- the size of a wedding dress (or a wedding veil, or a royal train on a wedding dress)
- the amount of material needed to make a man's three-piece suit
- the length of a maharajah's ceremonial sash
- the length of a standard bolt of cloth
- the length of a burial shroud
- the length of cloth needed for a Scottish "great kilt"
- the nine yards of lanolin-soaked wool blankets the early Scots would wrap themselves in
- the length of Indian saris used for weddings and special occasions
- the length of turbans mandated under British colonial rule so that all castes would be equally outfitted
- the length of animal skins needed to cover a tepee

Some of these may be dismissed because they predate the 1960s. Then there's the fact that one size does not fit all. Depending on an individual's height and weight, the material for a garment may be anywhere from four to seven yards. The standard bolt of cloth is much longer than nine yards, the average kilt takes about five yards of material, and there never was a mandated standard for turban size. Most of these explanations, in other words, do not reflect facts. And even if a sash were actually nine yards long, what does fashion have to do with the meaning "all of it"? Any total length would fit the bill; nine yards would have no special claim.

Some explanations are rather bellicose in nature, claiming military origins.

- the bullet clips for Gatling guns (or some other WW I machine gun) were nine yards long
- 50 calibre machine gun ammunition belts in WW II Supermarine Spitfires measured exactly 27 feet (variations: the Corsair fighter, the B-17, the P-47)
- a three-masted warship had three yardarms on each mast for the square sails, making nine in all

- traditionally, newly promoted sailors in the British Navy had to make the rounds of nine designated pubs near the London docks, drinking a "yard" of ale at each
- nine yards was the amount of material needed to make a parachute
- a soldier's pack had a nine-yard capacity

In all six explanations, the era is wrong. In addition, the gun's manufacturer varies from account to account, and separate clips seem to have been eleven feet long. In warships, anywhere from fifteen to eighteen yardarms were not uncommon. British paratroopers used a chute which was just short of eight yards in diameter. So all of these seem to be shot down with a minimum of research.

Wheeled vehicles form another category used to account for the phrase's origin. Thus, we have

- the capacity of a West Virginia ore wagon
- the volume of rubbish that would fill a standard garbage truck
- the capacity of a ready-mix cement truck
- the capacity of a horse-drawn coal wagon

In the 1960s, when the first written use of the phrase appears, cement trucks held 6+ cubic yards of material. Garbage trucks come in all different sizes. A Ford cabover garbage truck had a 20 yard capacity, for instance, and a Peterbilt Heil had a 31 yard capacity. The ore and coal wagons are in the wrong time frame.

One of the more likely sources for the phrase is the game of American football, where ten-yard segments are quite significant. If the phrase were the whole ten yards, I would yell Bingo! and collect my prize, but how do we explain something which comes up short? I have seen two explanations:

- this is a sarcastic reference to sloppy measurements by early football referees before chains were mandated
- it is a sarcastic euphemism used by football coaches for failure: you used all that energy and still fell short—you went

the whole nine yards when you needed ten to make a first down

Then there are the explanations that range from the bizarre to the outrageous to the totally irrelevant. They're my favorites.

- The length of a hangman's noose
- The distance between the inner and outer fences of a prison
- The volume of a rich man's deep grave during the Black Plague
- The whole nine yards was based upon the nine Fora of the Ancient Philosophers. A principle had to be validated in all nine Fora (courtyards used for debate); for the idea to be accepted, it went the whole nine yards.
- A phrase used by doctors meaning the 27 feet of small intestine (actually, in an adult they are about 20 feet long)
- Variation of above: medieval disembowelment practices which exposed the alleged 27 feet of small intestine
- Painters used to measure large quantities of paint by the area it could cover. The common unit was set at nine yards.
- The length of an old-fashioned manual typewriter ribbon; a really long typed report went the whole nine yards
- The number of properties, or yards, in a standard city block
- Derived from the handicapping system in the now defunct sport of live pigeon (trap) shooting

So there you have it, all of the definitive origins for the whole nine yards herded together in one corral. If you have one of your own which is not listed, be sure to pass it on. And if you can find an authenticated written use which predates 1967, you'll be wined and dined by the linguistic community.

What's that? You want to know what my take is? Out of modesty, I have held back, but if you insist….

- The 10th letter of the Phoenician alphabet was called yodh. (Incidentally, this letter was also absorbed into the Hebrew alphabet.) It was forbidden by punishment of death for a commoner to say the sacred name of the king aloud, so it was always written. To write the phrase "King Nebuchadnezzar of Babylon" you had to use nine yodhs. Hence the phrase, "the whole nine yodhs," a coded reference to his unspeakable name, which became corrupted over the centuries into yards. A Syrian colleague of mine assures me that this is absolutely true.

Note: Since this was originally written, researcher Barry Popik has uncovered what he considers a likely source. He thinks it comes from an off-color joke about a drunken Scotsman who knits a very long scarf for his betrothed. When he delivers the gift late one night, he is inebriated and naked from the waist down. As he talks about the scarf, his beloved thinks that he is talking about his exposed parts.

See www.barrypopik.com/article/880/the-scotsmans-kilt

MALAPROPISMS AND MONDEGREENS

One of the delights of language is the unintentional mistake. No, it's not delightful to the writer or speaker—it's a delight to the reader or hearer. Consider this example: "She was invested with lice." My first response is to picture bloodsucking stockbrokers taking advantage of some hapless investor. Then reality kicks in, and I realize that the word should have been infested.

Mistakes such as this can happen either of two ways: actively or passively. In an active situation, the speaker or writer is overtly reaching for a word to express a meaning when the process goes awry. There might be many reasons for this: an individual's habitual misuse of a particular word, a word whose definition has been derived solely from sketchy context, two words that bear a superficial resemblance to each other (whether visually or aurally), a perverse tendency to value polysyllabic words over simpler but adequate terms, and so on. In a passive situation, the speaker or writer is a recipient. He or she mishears a word and reproduces it as it sounded. On the part of the listener, inattention, interference, or a hearing disorder may be to blame; on the part of the speaker, bad enunciation.

A malapropism is an example of the active process. The name comes from Mrs. Malaprop, a character in Richard Brinsely Sheridan's play, The Rivals (1775). While this type of error also deliberately appeared in works such as Much Ado About Nothing, Joseph Andrews, and Humphrey Clinker, Mrs. Malaprop really nailed it, and so she has become the eponym of record. Her name, by the way, came from the French mal à propos—inappropriate or out of place. Here are some examples of her word mangling:

- "I would by no means wish a daughter of mine to be a progeny of learning." [prodigy]
- "She should have a supercilious knowledge in accounts...." [superficial]
- "...she should know something of the contagious countries...." [contiguous]
- "...and likewise that she might reprehend the true meaning of what she is saying." [apprehend]
- "...I don't think there is a superstitious article in it." [superfluous]
- "She's as headstrong as an allegory on the banks of the Nile." [alligator]
- "He is the very pineapple of politeness." [pinnacle]
- "...a nice derangement of epitaphs." [arrangement of epithets]
- "...illiterate him, I say, quite from your memory." [obliterate]
- "Now don't attempt to extirpate yourself from the matter..." [extricate]
- "Ah! few gentlemen, now-a-days, know how to value the ineffectual qualities in a woman!" [intellectual]
- "...long ago I laid my positive conjunctions on her, never to think on the fellow again." [injunctions]
- "Behold, this very day, I have interceded another letter from the fellow." [intercepted]
- "No caparisons, miss, if you please." [comparisons]
- "I am sorry to say, Sir Anthony, that my affluence over my niece is very small." [influence]
- "O mercy!—I'm quite analyzed, for my part!" [amazed]
- "...and Sir Anthony not to be found to prevent the antistrophe!" [catastrophe]
- "...but he can tell you the perpendiculars." [particulars]
- "O fy! it would be very inelegant in us:—we should only participate things." [precipitate]
- "Come, girls! this gentleman will exhort us." [escort]

Well over 200 years later, malapropisms still protuberate ...er... proliferate. They go by many names (*gaffe, slip of the tongue, blooper, bushism, eggcorn, catachresis*), and they come in many varieties, but they are always funny. In fact, comedians such as Norm Crosby built entire careers on them.

- "Every home should have a fire distinguisher."
- "It is cheaper to send a package by partial post."
- "The search is on for the abdominal snowman."
- "A forest stranger leads a very lonely life."
- "Yuri Geller claims to have extra-century perception."
- "The flood damage was so bad they had to evaporate the city."
- "Don't make decisions on the sperm of the moment."
- "She's sitting in the preverbial catbird seat."
- "This is totally beyond my apprehension."
- "We cannot let terrorists and rogue nations hold this nation hostile."
- "Republicans understand the importance of bondage between a mother and child."
- "I am mindful not only of preserving executive powers for myself, but for my predecessors as well."

I spoke earlier about a passive process that results in unintentional mistakes. This one is based on mishearing, and we'll get to its classic form, the mondegreen, in just a moment. Meanwhile, to act as a transition, let's take a look at some mistaken words and phrases that are showing up frequently in print, in speech, on the internet, and anywhere else where popular communication is common.

I've never seen confirmation from the Apple Corporation itself, but a web site at Stanford University passes along the story that a speech recognition software team at that company made up T-shirts that read, "I helped Apple wreck a nice beach." Before you reach for your ecology banners, try saying that quickly a few times. You'll discover that it comes out as, "I helped Apple recognize speech." This illustrates the process that transmutes sounds spelled one way into another spelling that more or less preserves the original sound, but distorts the original meaning. Remember the bumper sticker, "Visualize Whirled Peas"? Here are more examples.
- Old timer's disease
     Alzheimer's disease
- For all intensive purposes
     For all intents and purposes
- A soft dancer turneth away wrath
     A soft answer turneth away wrath

- At your beckon call
  - At your beck and call
- Butt naked
  - Buck naked
- Calm, cool, and collective
  - Calm, cool, and collected
- Chester drawers
  - Chest of drawers
- Chicken feet
  - Chicken feed
- Chicken pops
  - Chicken pox
- Day of sex machina
  - Deus ex machina
- Deep-seeded fear
  - Deep-seated fear
- Diabolically opposed
  - Diametrically opposed
- Dire straights
  - Dire straits
- Escape goat
  - Scape goat
- Heart rendering
  - Heart rending
- He drank himself into Bolivia
  - He drank himself into oblivion
- In tack
  - Intact
- It's a blessing in the sky
  - It's a blessing in disguise
- It's a doggy-dog world
  - It's a dog-eat-dog world
- Lack toast and tolerance
  - Lactose intolerant
- Momento
  - Memento
- New leash on life
  - New lease on life
- No holes barred
  - No holds barred

- One in the same
  - One and the same
- Open sores software
  - Open source software
- Out of arm's sway
  - Out of harm's way
- Palpitated my abdomen
  - Palpated my abdomen
- Paper-view TV
  - Pay-per-view TV
- Piping hot ethnic muffins
  - Piping hot Egg McMuffins
- Praying on the innocent
  - Preying on the innocent
- Reign him in
  - Rein him in
- Slight of hand
  - Sleight of hand
- Smoking mirrors
  - Smoke and mirrors
- Something or rather
  - Something or other
- Sorted past
  - Sordid past
- Take it for granite
  - Take it for granted
- The Rose on Walden Pond
  - Thoreau's Walden Pond
- Tongue and cheek
  - Tongue in cheek
- Tough road to hoe
  - Tough row to hoe
- Tow the line
  - Toe the line
- Very close veins
  - Varicose veins

Then, of course, there's that invaluable lifesaving procedure when someone is choking on food: the Hind Lick Maneuver.

Strictly speaking, a mondegreen is a misheard song lyric. Author Sylvia Wright coined the term. As a child, while listening to a Scottish ballad, she thought a line said, "They hae slain the Earl of Murray, and Lady Mondegreen." Years later, after much misplaced sympathy for the murdered Lady Mondegreen, she discovered that the line actually read, "They hae slain the Earl of Murray and laid him on the green."

It's easy to see why song lyrics are particularly susceptible to misunderstanding. The music can be loud, overwhelming, distracting. The singer is often screaming at the top of his lungs; otherwise, he's mumbling into the microphone to simulate intimacy. In the interests of sounding cool, he or she will often sacrifice proper enunciation for dialectical authenticity. The problem is that the way the brain is constructed, if some of the lyrics don't make sense, the listener feels compelled to supply something that at least *could* be what the singer said. Something is better than nothing.

Let's run through some of these misheard song lyrics to set the record straight.

Bob Dylan: "Dead ants are my friends, they're blowin' in the wind."
"The answers, my friend, are blowin' in the wind."

Johnny Rivers: "Secret Asian man"
"Secret agent man"

Evita: "Don't cry for me, Marge and Tina."
"Don't cry for me, Argentina."

Don Henley: "After the poison summer have gone"
"After the boys of summer have gone"

Bewitched, Bothered and Bewildered: "I'm wild again, defiled again, a simple and wintering child again."
I'm wild again, beguiled again, a simpering, whimpering child again."

America the Beautiful: ". . . from sea to Chinese sea"
   ". . .   *From sea to shining sea*"
   ``Oh, beautiful for spaceship guys"
      "Oh, beautiful for spacious skies"

Creedence Clearwater Revival:"There's a bathroom on the right"   *"There's a bad moon on the rise"*

Julie London: "Crimean River."
   "Cry me a river"

Sousa march: "Tarzan Strikes Forever"
   "Stars and stripes forever"

Robert Palmer: "I've got a backache from loving you"
   "I've got a bad case of loving you"

Hoyt Axton: "Joy to officials in the deep blue sea"
   "'Joy to the fishes in the deep blue sea"

Eric Clapton: "Won't you be my four-level woman? I want to be your four-level man"
   "Won't you be my forever woman? I want to be your forever man"

The Beatles: ``Will you still need me, will you still feed me, when I'm 6 feet 4?"
   "Will you still need me, will you still feed me, when I'm sixty-four?"
   "The girl with colitis goes by"
   "The girl with kaleidoscope eyes"

"She's got a tic in her eye"
   "She's got a ticket to ride"

Crystal Gayle: "Doughnuts Make Your Brown Eyes Blue"
   "Don't it make your brown eyes blue?"

Paul Young: "Every time you go away you take a piece of meat with you"
   "Every time you go away you take a piece of me with you"

Maria Muldaur: "Midnight After You're Wasted"
"Midnight at the oasis."

Swing Low: "Swing low, sweet cherry yacht"
"Swing low, sweet chariot"

Chicago: "If she would have been paid for"
"If she would have been faithful"

Simon and Garfunkel: "Silence like a casserole"
"Silence like a cancer grows"

Herman's Hermits: "There's a can of fish all over the world tonight."
"There's a kind of hush all over the world tonight."

Pink Floyd: "No dogs orgasm in the classroom"
"No dark sarcasm in the classroom"

Angel of the Morning: "Just brush my teeth before you leave me, baby"
"Just brush my cheek before you leave me, baby"

ZZ Top: Everybody's crazy 'bout a shot glass man
"Everybody's crazy 'bout a sharp-dressed man"

Christmas carols seem to be a particularly prolific source of mondegreens. They're heard only one short season every year, and many choirs lack perfect enunciation, so I suppose it shouldn't come as a surprise. In addition, many of the mistaken lyrics are reported by children.

"Rudolph the red-nosed reindeer had a very Chinese nose"
"Rudolph the red-nosed reindeer had a very shiny nose"

"Olive, the other reindeer"
"All of the other reindeer"

"You'll go down and kiss Doreen!"
"You'll go down in history!"
"Sleep in heavenly peas"

"Sleep in heavenly peace"

"Bells on cocktails ring, making spareribs bright."
"Bells on bobtails ring, making spirits bright."

"Just like the wands I used to know"
"Just like the ones I used to know"

"I'm dreaming of a white Christmas with every Christian car
I ride"
*"I'm dreaming of a white Christmas with every Christmas card I
write"*

"Fleas, naughty dog"
"Feliz Navidad"

"On the first day of Christmas my tulip gave to me"
"On the first day of Christmas my true love gave to me"

"Later on we'll perspire, as we dream by the fire"
"Later on we'll conspire, as we dream by the fire"

"Santa Claus is scum in two towns"
"Santa Claus is comin' to town"

"He's makin' a list, chicken and rice"
"He's makin' a list, checkin' it twice"

"Noel. Noel, Barney's the king of Israel"
"Noel, Noel, Born is the king of Israel"

"In the meadow we can build a snowman, then pretend that
he is sparse and brown"
*"In the meadow we can build a snowman, then pretend that he is
Parson Brown"*

"The first Noel the angels did say was to serpents in shelters
in fields as they lay"
*"The first Noel the angels did say was to certain poor shepherds in
fields as they lay"*

"Chipmunks roasting on an open fire"
"Chestnuts roasting on an open fire"

"Where shepherds washed their socks by night"
"Where shepherds watched their flocks by night"

"Let us know, let us know, let us know"
"Let it snow, let it snow, let it snow"

"Holy infant sold tender and mild"
"Holy infant so tender and mild"

So there we are. Little did Lady Mondegreen know that she was going to launch a cottage industry on the internet when she perished along with the URL of moray.

MACH 1

To paraphrase lyricist Earl K. Brent,
War is
Where you find it
Don't be blind it's
All around you
Everywhere.

You slide into the passenger seat of a car, and your friend waits patiently while you fiddle with the seatbelt. The metal buckle to your right is incredibly elusive; you must grope repeatedly until your fingers close around it. Even when you find it, the retractor lets you pull the belt only part way to its goal, requiring you to seesaw repeatedly until you feel like you're getting a workout on a demented weight machine. The receptacle latch is hidden between the seats somewhere to your left, and it defiantly refuses to reward you with that soul-satisfying *click*.

You, my friend, are engaged in unholy kolymachy [*Gr. koly, restrain or inhibit*] + [*machy, battle*], and the driver's patience will undoubtedly give out before your heaving chest is finally strapped in.

George Orwell's legitimate observations to the contrary, there's something deeply satisfying about using sesquipedalian words occasionally, but -*machy* is a word part which must fight to get the attention that it deserves. Ultimately, the noun came from the Greek verb *machesthai*, to wage a battle. It shows up in two forms in English, -*machy* and -*machia*, and the hyphens indicate that those combining forms are meant to end a word.

While many -*machy* words bear the scars of ancient wars and serve mainly as historical reminders, verbivores will find them inherently interesting and will cull usable components for contemporary use. For instance, before PETA raised people's consciousness, the masses found staged animal fights enormously entertaining. They would flock to alectoromachy, cockfighting, [<*Gr. cock* + *fight*]; they could barely wait to participate in cynarctomachy, bear baiting with a dog, [<*Gr. dog* + *bear* + *fight*]; and they would herd together to watch tauromachy, bullfighting, [<*Gr. bull* + *fight*]. And unless ancient writers were just horsing around, fans in their day were treated to centauromachia, a battle in which centaurs take part, [<*Gr. centaur* + *battle*], and minotauromachy, a battle with a minotaur.

On a more lofty plane, theologians concerned themselves with gigantomachy, a war of giants, especially the fabulous war of the giants against heaven, [<*Gr. giant* + *battle*], iconomachy, hostility to images as objects of worship, [<*Gr. an image* + *fight*], pneumatomachy, denial of the divinity of the Holy Spirit, [<*Gr. spirit or breath* + *battle*], psychomachy, a conflict of the soul, [<*Gr. the soul* + *battle*], angelomachy, the conflict between good and bad angels, [<*Gr. angel* + *battle*], and theomachy, opposition to God or divine will, [<*Gr. a god* + *a battle*].

Back to earth again, literary types wrote of batrachomyomachy, the battle between the frogs and mice—a Greek parody on the Iliad, [<*Gr. frog* + *mouse* + *battle*], logomachy, a dispute over or about words, [<*Gr. word* + *battle*], and poetomachia, a contest of poets, [<*L. poet* + *Gr. battle*].

Other neglected -*machy* terms include monomachy, a duel, [<*Gr. single,* + *battle*], trimachy, a series of three battles [<*Gr. three* + *battle*], naumachy, a staged sea battle, [<*Gr. ship* + *battle*], chiromachy, hand-to hand combat [<*Gr. hand* + *battle*], pygmachy, boxing, [<*Gr. fist* + *battle*], symmachy, a fight against a common enemy, [<*Gr. alliance* + *battle*], and sciamachy, mock or futile combat, [<*Gr. shadow* + *battle*]. A strange one was ostomachy, a game played with fourteen pieces of bone [<*Gr. bone* + *battle*].

But to keep from wallowing in nostalgia, perhaps we should update the -*machy* word hoard, as I did earlier with kolymachy, the neologistic battle of the belts. I don't know about you, but I seem to be at war with inanimate objects on a daily basis. Take telephone and appliance cords, for instance. I can't tell you how often they spiral out of control and resist my attempts to untwist them. It's outright funimachy [<*Gr. cord* + *battle*]. Then there are sweaters that refuse to fit over my head and coat sleeves that leap out of the way as my hands approach them. We're talking hesthomachy here, folks, [<*Gr. clothing* + *battle*]. No doubt many of you have also experienced clidomachy, especially coming home late at night. Fighting to get that key into the lock is as frustrating as it gets [<*Gr. key* + *battle*]. Millions of Americans are at war with weight gain [baromachy], while uncounted others struggle against addictions to smoking, drinking, or gambling [capnomachy, potomachy, and aleamachy]. And every couple I know engages in klinoskepasmamachy [*Gr. blanket* + *battle*] in the middle of a chilly night. I certainly hope I never have to say that word out loud.

I guess it's time to engage in phobomachy [<*Gr. fear* + *battle*] and to marshal the troops for another battle, though it's impossible to say whence it will come. Perhaps, like Oliver Goldsmith, we will find our strength in flexibility:

> "For he who fights and runs away
> May live to fight another day;
> But he who is in battle slain
> Can never rise and fight again."

HUE AND CRY

Sometimes, if you approach a dictionary with a spirit of hypersensitivity and deliberate soft focus, a dimensional shift takes place. At that moment, you sense an underlying air of desperation, smell the coppery odor of nervous perspiration, and see the rimless eyeglasses perched on the lexicographer's nose quivering in futility.

Nowhere is this more evident than in the attempt to define colors. After all, we are asking for the impossible: define something that only the eye can decipher, something ineluctably connected to light waves, but do it by using words exclusively. It's like trying to paint the interior of Plato's cave after the fire has burned out. We might as well attempt to compose music by using the palette of sweet, salt, sour, and bitter.

This is true even of the seven standard colors—the ones that splay their tinted fingers when light passes through a prism. Dictionary makers resort to a couple of indirect methods to define ROY G. BIV. Some give examples of familiar objects, hoping that the reader will picture them in their true colors. Others resort to science by invoking the spectrum and enumerating wavelengths. The truly desperate ones blither: they are reduced to repeating the name of the color, a violation of the canon that a definition shall not repeat the word being defined.

Let's start by observing how the venerable *Oxford English Dictionary, 1st Edition*, handled its impossible assignment. In traditional prismatic order, we find the following:

- RED: having, or characterized by, the colour which appears at the lower or least refracted end of the visible spectrum, and is familiar in nature as that of blood, fire, various flowers (as the poppy and rose), and ripe fruits (whence the frequent similes *red as blood, fire, a rose, cherry*, etc.).
- ORANGE: The reddish-yellow colour of the orange.
- YELLOW: The colour of gold, butter, the yolk of an egg, various flowers, and other objects; constituting one (the most luminous) of the primary colours, occurring in the spectrum between green and orange.
- GREEN: The colour which in the spectrum is intermediate between blue and yellow; in nature chiefly conspicuous as the colour of growing herbage and leaves.
- BLUE: The name of one of the colours of the spectrum; of the colour of the sky and of the deep sea; cerulean.
- INDIGO: The colour yielded by indigo, reckoned by Newton as one of the seven prismatic or primary colours, lying in the spectrum between blue and violet, and now often called blue-violet or violet-blue.
- VIOLET: A purplish-blue colour resembling that of the violet.

Obviously, James Murray chose the exemplification route, and in spite of his talent and dedication, you can see the shortcomings. For one thing, there can be no set and invariable color connected with each object. Time of day, season of the year, light source, production methods, individual perceptions, and a host of other considerations enter in. For another, values such as hue, brightness, and saturation are glossed over. Thus, if we already know our colors, these definitions will evoke useful memories, but they teach us nothing directly. A visitor from Mars would be left scratching its heads.

Now let's take a look at a more scientific approach, this one embraced by *American Heritage Dictionary, 4th Edition*:

- RED: The hue of the long-wave end of the visible spectrum, evoked in the human observer by radiant energy with wavelengths of approximately 630 to 750 nanometers.
- ORANGE: The hue of that portion of the visible spectrum

lying between red and yellow, evoked in the human observer by radiant energy with wavelengths of approximately 590 to 630 nanometers.

• YELLOW: The hue of that portion of the visible spectrum lying between orange and green, evoked in the human observer by radiant energy with wavelengths of approximately 570 to 590 nanometers.

• GREEN: The hue of that portion of the visible spectrum lying between yellow and blue, evoked in the human observer by radiant energy with wavelengths of approximately 490 to 570 nanometers.

• BLUE: The hue of that portion of the visible spectrum lying between green and indigo, evoked in the human observer by radiant energy with wavelengths of approximately 420 to 490 nanometers.

• INDIGO: The hue of that portion of the visible spectrum lying between blue and violet, evoked in the human observer by radiant energy with wavelengths of approximately 420 to 450 nanometers.

• VIOLET: The hue of the short-wave end of the visible spectrum, evoked in the human observer by radiant energy with wavelengths of approximately 380 to 420 nanometers.

This is a no-nonsense and scrupulously accurate account, one with far more parallelism and uniformity than the *OED*'s effort, but I can't picture a thing. In this case, science produces a washed-out canvas if no prism or color chart is at hand.

The Random House Dictionary, 2nd Edition, blends these two approaches:

• RED: Any of various colors resembling the color of blood; the primary color at one extreme end of the visible spectrum, an effect of light with a wavelength between 610 and 780 nm.

• ORANGE: A color between yellow and red in the spectrum, an effect of light with a wavelength between 590 and 610 nm.

• YELLOW: A color like that of egg yolk, ripe lemons, etc.; the primary color between green and orange in the visible spectrum, an effect of light with a wavelength between 570 and 590 nm.

• GREEN: A color intermediate in the spectrum between yellow and blue, an effect of light with a wavelength between 500 and 570 nm.

• BLUE: The pure color of a clear sky; the primary color between green and violet in the visible spectrum, an effect of light with a wavelength between 450 and 500 nm.

- INDIGO: A color ranging from a deep violet blue to a dark, grayish blue. [An editor was asleep at the color wheel here.]
- VIOLET: Reddish blue, a color at the opposite end of the visible spectrum from red, an effect of light with a wavelength between 400 and 450 nm.

I am not a cruel man, but let's follow this thread through two more examples and observe the beads of sweat forming on worried editorial brows:

Webster's Revised Unabridged Dictionary, 1913 Edition:

- RED: Of the color of blood, or of a tint resembling that color; of the hue of that part of the rainbow, or of the solar spectrum, which is furthest from the violet part.
- ORANGE: The color of an orange; reddish yellow.
- YELLOW: Being of a bright saffronlike color; of the color of gold or brass; having the hue of that part of the rainbow, or of the solar spectrum, which is between the orange and the green.
- GREEN: Having the color of grass when fresh and growing; resembling that color of the solar spectrum which is between the yellow and the blue; verdant; emerald.
- BLUE: Having the color of the clear sky, or a hue resembling it, whether lighter or darker; as, the deep, blue sea; as blue as a sapphire; blue violets.
- INDIGO: A dark, dull blue color like the indigo of commerce.
- VIOLET: The color of a violet, or that part of the spectrum farthest from red. It is the most refrangible part of the spectrum.

Here, familiar examples dominate, with an occasional nod at the spectrum thrown in.

The Century Dictionary and Cyclopedia:

- RED: A color more or less resembling that of blood or the lower end of the spectrum.
- ORANGE: [*Surprisingly, no direct definition; it supplies many categories of orange instead.*]
- YELLOW: [*No direct definition; it supplies many categories of yellow instead.*]

- GREEN: The color of ordinary foliage; the color seen in the solar spectrum between wavelengths 0.511 and 0.543 micron.
- BLUE: The color of the clear sky or of natural ultramarine, or a shade or a tint resembling it.
- INDIGO: The violet-blue color of the spectrum, extending, according to Helmholtz, from G two-thirds of the way to F in the prismatic spectrum.
- VIOLET: A general class of colors, of which the violet-flower is a highly chromatic example.

I love that "highly chromatic example"; you can almost hear the flip-flap of little weasel feet.

Allow me to end this phase of my musings with a final example, this one from the *Longman Dictionary of Contemporary English*:

- RED: The colour of blood or fire; see picture on page 411.
- ORANGE: A colour that is between red and yellow; see picture on page 413.
- YELLOW: The colour of butter, gold, or the middle part of an egg; see picture on page 411.
- GREEN: The colour of grass or leaves; see picture on page 411.
- BLUE: The colour of a clear sky or of the sea on a fine day; see picture on page 411.
- INDIGO: A dark purplish blue colour.
- VIOLET: A colour between purple and blue; see picture on page 411.

This is a down-to-earth editor. In effect, any pretense that this is a job for words has been jettisoned, and we are directed (except for one lapse) to visuals. I sense a fellow parent behind the scenes. This is, after all, the way we taught our own children. In the car or at the supermarket, we pointed to objects and declared their color. Once the tyke successfully began to associate a color with its name, we moved on to other lessons.

As we leave the prismatic colors and move on to amalgams of color, the basic vocabulary is now in place. Hue, saturation, and brightness become players, but at this stage subjectivity begins to paint with a broad brush.

Take the color ecru. Its definitions can be maddening.

- A grayish to pale yellow or light grayish-yellowish brown. — *American Heritage Dictionary, 4th Edition*
- A variable color averaging light grayish-yellowish brown; a pale to grayish yellow. — *Merriam-Webster Dictionary, 11th Edition*
- Very light brown in color, as raw silk, unbleached linen, etc. — *Random House Dictionary, 2nd Edition*
- Light-yellowish brown. — *Funk & Wagnalls New Practical Standard Dictionary*
- Very light brown. — *Hyperdictionary Online*
- The colour of unbleached linen. — *Oxford English Dictionary, 1st Edition*
- Having the color of raw silk, or of undyed and unbleached linen; hence, by extension, having any similar shade of neutral color, as the color of hemp or hempen cord. — *The Century Dictionary and Cyclopedia*

In French, écru meant unbleached or raw, but we can see from these examples that unbleached linen and raw silk are not everywhere perceived alike.

Then there's the color taupe, which comes from the Latin *talpa*, "a mole." Unfortunately, a mole's fur does not have an invariable color, so that leads to some fuzziness in the definitions.

- A brownish gray. — *American Heritage Dictionary, 4th Edition*
- A grayish brown. — *Wordnet Dictionary*
- A brownish gray. — *Merriam-Webster Dictionary, 11th Edition*
- Dark gray. — *Funk & Wagnalls New Practical Standard Dictionary*
- A moderate to dark brownish gray, sometimes slightly tinged with purple, yellow, or green. — *Random House Dictionary, 2nd Edition*

The prize for fuzziness, however, goes to fuscous, which comes from the Latin *fuscus*, "dusky." Bad sign: any word that starts out in the dark is not going to be very illuminating.

- Brown or grayish black; darkish. — *Webster's 1913 Dictionary*

• Dark brownish-gray. — *American Heritage Dictionary, 4th Edition*

• Any of several colors averaging a brownish gray. — *Merriam-Webster Dictionary, 11th Edition*

• Grayish-brown or tawny; dusky. — *Funk & Wagnalls New Practical Standard Dictionary*

• Dark in colour; tawny. — *Hutchinson Encyclopaedia*

• A color lighter than taupe, less strong than average chocolate, and slightly redder than mouse gray. — *Webster's Third New International*

Sidebar: since tawny came up twice above, let's take a quick look:

• Light brown or brownish orange. — *Wordnet*

• A dull yellowish brown color, like things tanned, or persons who are sunburnt. — *Webster's 1913 Dictionary*

• A light yellowish brown colour, like that of a lion. — *Cambridge Advanced Learner's Dictionary*

None of this is meant to denigrate lexicographers. Actually, I think it brave of them to attempt something that is doomed from the start by the nature of our senses. But it illustrates something about the translation of reality to words, and it serves as a warning that reliance on just one dictionary is not good practice. When it comes to color, it's certainly not a black-and-white matter.

And that's a good place to end — with an illustration that even black and white are not as set as first appears. In my *Word Parts Dictionary*, there is a section on word parts used to describe subtle color shadings, and black and white are included. Here are some word parts to describe the lack of reflected light and the reflection of nearly all light of all visible wavelengths.

Black

atro-	inky black	atroceruleus
ebon-	ebony black	ebonize
fulig-	sooty black	fuliginated
melan-	deep black	melanous
nigr-	blue black	nigrosine
piceo-	reddish black	piceo-ferruginous

White

alb-	standard white	albicant
alut-	leathery white	alutaceous
cand-	intense white	candescent
ceruss-	lead white	cerussal
ebur-	ivory white	eburnine
lac-	milk white	lacteous
leuco-	pale white	eucous
niv-	snow white	niveous
ochroleuc-	yellowish white	ochroleucous

Holy shades of meaning, Batman!

GUARDIAN|GUIDEWORDS

Guidewords are the two words that appear at the top of every dictionary page to indicate the first and the last entry to be found on that page.

Guidewords are sober, reliable, and unobtrusive to a fault. To the uninitiated, they are invisible. To the experienced dictionary user, they encourage speed reading to find the precise page on which a word resides.

The neophyte plods all the way through columns A and B on many successive pages before finding the word needed. The veteran skims through guidewords exclusively, ignoring the rest of the page until he or she pounces upon the only alphabetically viable pair.

Recently, I have stumbled upon a literary exercise—a game, really—that involves these sedate signposts. Into their otherwise drab and somber lives, this game introduces verve, humor, even frivolity. It allows them to trade in their charcoal gray suits for loud plaid. Giggles replace grunts, and wild dancing supplants stiff-backed sentry duty.

Most intriguing, this phenomenon involves serendipity and the sheer accident of juxtaposition. It is observed, not planned, because precisely which guidewords will appear at the top of a page depends solely on where headwords end up, and that is the result of typesetting considerations: type size and style, line spacing, line length, number of lines per page, column width, justification, and so on. Thus, no two dictionaries will have the same guidewords. This is aleatory writing at its purest.

Consider these examples from a dictionary pulled at random from my bookshelf (American Heritage Dictionary, 1969 edition), and savor the effect that they will have on you.

morale morgue	minister mint
Assyriology astronaut	Beard beautiful
bellyband bend	sack saddle soap
reality principle rebel	precipitation predicament
T-bone teal	Anáhuac anarchism
unworldly Upper Canada	pornography portico
sexton shaft	bracket fungus brain
paddock paint	corruptible cosign
news agency nibble	recount recusant
rocking horse roguery	fiction field corn
glacier glass	truckload truss
dreamer drill	shipmaster shock
skylight slather	fourfold fox trot
pinch Pinkerton	sediment seep
frosting fry	funny bone fuse

I don't know about you, but I'm in the presence of poetry. The juxtapositions are ludicrous, jarring, humorous, unlikely, and insightful all at once. I experience a similar effect when I read Old English poetry and encounter compressed but mind-stretching figures such as whale-road, life-lord, glory-gain, root-hewn, moor-stepper, and sorrow-halls. The same feeling washes over me when Gerard Manley Hopkins writes of dare-gale skylarks, skies of couple-colour, wind-long fleeces, sinew-service, dapple-drawn-dawn Falcon, and the blood-gush blade-gash. The unexpected juxtaposition, the powerful alliteration, and the arresting assonance can cause us to widen our eyes, catch our breath, expand our imagination, and finally expel an appreciative Ahhhhh! through smiling lips.

So just what are we supposed to do with these dynamic duos? Some players prefer to weave amusing guidewords into microstories:

"Tom drove through the **Haverford haze**, using the **bay beacon** to avoid making a **turkey turn** into the **martial law marsh**. He was on his way to the **Celt center**, and though he was not looking forward to encountering **charter member chatter** from the **close call clown,** the **detestable developer,** or the **etiquette eunuch,** he did have to face the **cudgel culture** of that **insoluble institutionalism.** He had to get the **lead pencil lease** signed or suffer a vicious **birthstone bite.** No one could get more **cabin boy cacophonous** than his **lampost landowner,** so Tom was worried."

I, however, prefer to go the pseudo-poetry route. The poem may employ wretched rhyme, as in the following two examples.

INFINITESIMAL INFORMATION

Infinitesimal information;
                  Mockery modification.
Laboratory lacrimation:
                  Ruffled grouse rumination
   and
                  Collie colonization.
Concupiscence condonation:
                  Venus's-hair verification

GLACIER GLASS

Glacier glass,
Dingbat dip.
Partnership pass,
Fleury flip.
Field day fight,
Factual faint.
Life insurance light,
Paddock paint.
Deceitful deck,
Flaming flat.
Neapolitan neck,
Scanty scat.
Dreamer drill.
Pigeon breast pill.

Alternatively, you might use a theme to aid in your selections. That will probably force you to jettison any rhyme scheme unless the warden frequently encourages you to engage in busy work.

ANIMAL ANIMUS

Backstay badger, barker barracuda.
Blender blister-beetle, bumblebee buoy.
Burr bush pig, calculated calf.
Carmine carp, cathead Caucasoid.
Caucasus cavefish, channel bass char.
Collie colonization, customable cuttlefish.
Dominance donkey, dormouse double.
Enfeeble English setter, English sheepdog enmity.
Eraser ermine, firepower fish.
Ghastly gibbon, Gilead giraffe.
Grass snake graviton, horizontal horse.
Horseback hospitality, Jack Frost jaguar.
Klipspringer knitting, lamb lampoon.
Mongoose monochrome, palladous palomino.
Picturesque pigeon, pinkeye pinyon jay.
Puff adder pulp, punctilious puppy.
Puppyish purple, reportage reptile.
Reptilian resect, ruffled grouse rumination.
Scorpion fish scowl, sheepdog shelter.
Southern bug sow, sowbelly spangle.
Tiger moth timbre, toadfish toga.
Turkey turn, walrus wanting.
Wooly bear workbook.

GRAMMAR GRANDEUR

Antler aorist, Archaic Latin archives.
Exclamation point executive, generally genitive.
Parry Islands participle, particle partner.
Personal pronoun peruse, philosophical phonics.
Predicate preferable, pressroom preterite.
Sincere singular, topic sentence toroid.

RELIGION REMATCH

Agape aggressive, bank baptistery.
Church Slavonic cinchonism, crock cross.
Episcopal epoxy, faint-hearted faithful.
Faith healer fall, flagellant flammable.
Frankincense freckle, frightening frock.
Heavenly hectic, hydromedusa hymn.
Immaculate Conception impact, irremovable Islam.
Mahatma mail-order house, minister mint.
Pontiff pope, Pope porkpie.
Provisory psalm, pulpit punctilio.
Theatergoer theology.

MEDICINE MEDITATION

Alternate angle alveolar, alveolate amber.
Anecdonic angina, Belial bellyache.
Blood group blow, bodacious boil.
Broader bronchi, carcinoma careful.
Careless carminative, carpal carry.
Catabolism catch, chondrocranium chorus.
Corpus striatum corrupt, coveralls coxalgia.
Cripple crock, delivery room dementia.
Dipsomania dirty, disc discomformity.
Dramamine dream, embellishment embryo.
Embryogenesis Emmy, extensometer extraction.
Factual faint, fatal faucal.
Fossorial four-flusher, gamogenesis gape.
Headphone heart attack, heartbeat heaven.
Hospitalization hour, intestinal interference.
Jawbone jeopardy, laboratory lacrimation.
Moribund mortal, orderly organ.
Orifice orogeny, orthoscope osmosis.
Pill pincers, posttraumatic potential.
Sitter skeleton, speeding spermatogonium.
Spirited spleen, stomach pump stop.
Swamp boat sweat, thoracic thrash.
Tuck tumescent, tumid Tunisia.
Warlord wart, xerophilous xyster.

All of this has no socially redeeming value or academic significance whatsoever. It is simply language at play. Actually, I don't even know if there's a name for this diversion. A friend has suggested the term juxtapositionyms, and until I learn otherwise, that seems to cover the territory.

If you are going to play this guideword game, be prepared to let go of your **deep defense mechanism** and any **betwixt bias** that you may have. Try to avoid any **compilation complication** or **conferee conflict.** Whether you live in the **cordon bleu Corn Belt** or somewhere on the **Hoosier horizon,** and whether you're a **flying saucer fogy,** a **middle age midshipman,** or a **wanton warlock,** sharpen your **pellitory pencil** and keep your **evidence exact. Perception perfect** is the goal as you write your **repeated report**.

And when you get bored by this game, there's always **deckchair decoupage.**

OLLIE, OLLIE, -OLOGIST

Danish physicist Niels Bohr defined an expert as "Someone who has made all the mistakes that can be made, but in a very narrow field." In an age where word inflation makes it mandatory to use the term "expert" on every resumé, no matter how humble the position being sought (consider hamburgerologist), the word has lost its usefulness.

But as someone who is fascinated by names themselves, I find myself worrying less about individual authenticity and delighting more in terminology. The sheer number of names for experts is astounding. Many of them end in the combining form -ologist, a descendant of a Greek word meaning to speak—in this case, to speak with authority. For instance, here are some fields:
- tea expert (tsiologist)
- a swamp and bog expert (telmatologist)
- a truffles expert (hydnologist)
- a dream expert (oneirologist)
- a beard expert (pogonologist)

Expect to hear esoteric terms from these people:

- filicologist (ferns)
- carpologist (fruit and seed)
- an axiologist (values)
- a philematologist (kissing)

Of course, if you find yourself unable to pucker your lips properly, you may have to visit a stomatologist instead (diseases of the mouth).

Some fields of endeavor seem to invite sesquipedalian names more than others. The field of medicine is certainly one, and the subcategory disease is enough to turn anyone into a hypochondriac.

- paleopathologist specializes in ancient diseases
- paedonosologist focuses on children's diseases
- geopathologist considers the distribution of diseases
- loimologists (plagues)
- phthisiologists (tuberculosis)
- helcologists (ulcers)
- and rhinologists (nose)

Speaking of rhinos, this doesn't stop with humans; it extends to animals, too. So we find experts in animal pathogens (epizoologists) and in diseases of lower animals (zoopathologists).

These disease specialties get quite specific according to the creatures being studied, as this sampling shows:

- horses (hippopathologists)
- apes (pithecopathologists)
- dogs (cynopathologists)
- fish (icthyopathologists)
- snakes (herpetopathologists)
- whales (cetopathologists).

It's difficult to be at ease when the world holds so much illness. Why, phytopathologists will tell you that even plants are at risk.

Science aside, another field that revels in fancy names is religion. It's quite apparent what angelologists, diabologists, satanologists, demonologists, Buddhologists, hymnologists, christologists, martyrologists, sermonologists, Mariologists, and bibliologists specialize in, but other terms require a bit of meditation.

- pantheologist: all religions
- naologist: church buildings
- ponologist: evil
- pisteologist: faith
- patrologist: Fathers of the ancient church
- agathologist: goodness
- tartarologiswt: Hell
- heresiologist: heresies

- thaumatologists: miracles
- missiologists: missionary activity
- doxologists: praise of God
- lipsanologists: relics
- eschatologists: the four final events of life (death, judgment, heaven or hell)
- heortologists: religious calendars and feast days
- hagiologists: saints' lives
- pneumatologists: Holy Spirit

Now I know what monks do in their spare time.

While we are hovering in the celestial sphere, we may as well look at some terms relating to weather. Everyone talks about the weather, as the old saw goes, but you must know the terminology to participate on a more rarified level. We're all familiar with meteorologists from news programs, so we already know that their task is to describe atmospheric conditions. Not as well known are those who work behind the scenes and never appear on TV. Their specialties include:

- clouds (nephologists)
- sun spots and their effect on weather (heliologists)
- thunder (brontologists)
- wind conditions (anemologists)
- tornadoes (lilapsologists)
- snow and ice conditions (cryologists)
- atmospheric dust (coniologists)

There are even hardy souls who study climate conditions from thousands of years ago; they call themselves paleoclimatologists. And you thought that yesterday's weather was old news.

Food experts abound, too. Crithologists know all about barley, and agronomists study crop culture. Pomologists are interested in fruit; and that field breaks down into subspecialties:

- botyologists: grapes
- baccatologists: berries,
- sycologists: figs,
- piriologists: pears,
- persicologists: peaches,
- fragarologists: strawberries.

Lachanologists specialize in vegetables; I wonder if they all like broccoli. In turn there are subspecialties.
- brassicologists: cabbages
- spicologists: corn
- cucumologists: cucumbers
- phaseologists: kidney beans
- raphanologists: radishes
- napologists: turnips

Nuts are not exempt, either.
- acorns (balanologists)
- almonds (amygdalogists)
- cashews (anacardologists)
- chestnuts (castanologists)
- hickories (cichorologists)
- peanuts (arachologists)
- walnuts (juglandologists)

I should also put in a plug for language experts. Silent and unassuming for the most part, they live the truth of Ludwig Wittgenstein's observation every day of their lives: "The limits of my language means the limits of my world." [Tractatus] In their effort to expand the horizons of language, they have divided communication into specialties such as these:

- acrologist: alphabet formation
- alphabetologist: alphabet systems
- brachylogist: concise writing
- cacologist: incorrect diction
- chirologist: sign language
- cryptologist: coded language
- dactylologist: sign language
- dialectologist: dialects
- etymologist: word history
- glottochronologist: language evolution
- glottologist: linguistics
- graphologist: handwriting
- idiomologist: idioms
- lexicologist: application of words
- morphologist: language structure
- onomasiologist: grouped words

- onomatologist: proper names
- orthologist: correct use of words
- orismologist: technical terms
- philologist: language
- phonologist: speech sounds
- phraseologist: word order
- semasiologist: semantics
- terminologist: nomenclature
- tropologist: figurative language

Looking this partial list over, I must say that wordsmiths seem to be a verbose lot.

So whether you agree with Virgil ("Believe an expert") or with Nicholas Murray Butler ("An expert is one who knows more and more about less and less"), they are here to stay, along with their polysyllabic titles. Oddly enough, I didn't come across a term for an expert on experts in my readings, so I suppose I'll have to commit a neologism. I know this will offend purists who insist that Greek elements may be joined only with other Greek elements, but peritologist [L. peritus, expert] is a succinct and euphonious way to express it.

IRISH BULLS

- If Queen Victoria were alive today, she'd be turning over in her grave.
- May you never live to see your wife a widow.
- I'd give my right arm to be ambidextrous.

If you think running with the bulls at Pamplona is dangerous, look over your shoulder: here come the Irish Bulls!

The American Heritage Dictionary defines an Irish Bull as a statement containing an incongruity or a logical absurdity, usually unbeknownst to the speaker. As an example, it gives, "With a pistol in each hand and a sword in the other ... ."

Irish Bulls were deeply ingrained in the speech patterns of Sir Boyle Roche, a member of Parliament in various Irish counties from 1776 to 1800, and that's where the Irish connection comes in. The term was frozen in place by Dr John Mahaffy, a 19th Century scholar at Trinity College, Dublin. Asked what makes Irish bulls different from other bulls, he was quoted as saying, "An Irish Bull is always pregnant," making it superior, one supposes, to less prolific bovines in other lands.

Here are a few of the unforgettable utterances of good old boy Boyle:

- Why should we put ourselves out of our way to do anything for posterity? For what has posterity ever done for us?
- How can I be in two places at once, unless I were a bird?

- The cup of Ireland's misery has been overflowing for centuries and is not yet half full.
- Ireland and England are like two sisters; I would have them embrace like one brother.
- All along the untrodden paths of the future, I can see the footprints of an unseen hand.
- We should silence anyone who opposes the right to freedom of speech.
- The only thing to prevent what's past is to put a stop to it before it happens.
- At present there are such goings-on that everything is at a standstill.
- PS If you do not receive this, of course it must have been miscarried; therefore I beg you to write and let me know.

It takes your breath away, doesn't it? These incongruous statements are the result of pomposity, a tongue that moves faster than the cerebral cortex, and a blending of unblendable elements.

Over the course of time, Irish bulls were exported to other nations—the herd shot 'round the world, as it were—and we soon find them in America. One of the best-known practitioners of the art was Samuel Goldwyn, movie producer (1882-1974), though it is hard to say whether he or Yogi Berra should stand on the winner's pedestal.

A word of warning: though many of the following Irish Bulls have been attributed time after time either to Sam or to Yogi, there is no doubt that some of the attributions are spurious. No single person could have uttered so many arresting statements in just one lifetime. In some cases, overzealous press agents—under the mantra that any kind of publicity is better than no publicity at all—planted carefully-crafted brain twisters. Others, written by unknowns, were attributed to famous people in order to give them recognition and staying power. And both men may have had enemies eager to make them look careless or ignorant. So, with that truth in blending out of the way, let's mooove to pen central.

IRISH BULLS ATTRIBUTED TO SAMUEL GOLDWYN

- An oral contract isn't worth the paper it's written on.
- They stayed away in droves.
- If I could drop dead right now, I'd be the happiest man alive.
- Our comedies are not to be laughed at.
- Gentlemen, listen to me slowly.
- Never make forecasts, especially about the future.
- I paid too much for it, but it's worth it.
- Let's have some new cliches.
- I don't care if it doesn't make a nickel. I just want every man, woman, and child in America to see it.
- I never liked you and I always will.
- I'm willing to admit that I may not always be right, but I am never wrong.
- Give me a couple of years, and I'll make that actress an overnight success.
- It's absolutely impossible, but it has possibilities.
- A hospital is no place to be sick.
- Tell them to stand closer apart.
- Don't improve it into a flop!
- Anyone who goes to a psychiatrist ought to have his head examined.
- If you can't give me your word of honor, will you give me your promise?
- When I want your opinion I will give it to you.
- True, I've been a long time making up my mind, but now I'm giving you a definite answer. I won't say yes and I won't say no—but I'm giving you a definite maybe.

Hall of Famer Yogi Berra, legendary New York Yankees catcher and later manager of the Mets, felt compelled to write a book subtitled, *I really didn't say everything I said*, so we know that many of the sayings pinned on him were penned by someone else. Nevertheless, here are some

IRISH BULLS ATTRIBUTED TO YOGI BERRA

- This is like deja vu all over again.
- Baseball is 90% mental; the other half is physical.
- 90% of the putts that are short don't go in.
- You give 100 percent in the first half of the game, and if that isn't enough, in the second half you give what's left.
- If you can't imitate him, don't copy him.
- You should always go to other people's funerals; otherwise, they won't come to yours.
- If the fans don't come out to the ball park, you can't stop them.
- I always thought that record would stand until it was broken.
- Nobody goes there anymore; it's too crowded.
- It was impossible to get a conversation going; everybody was talking too much.
- You better cut the pizza in four pieces because I'm not hungry enough to eat six.
- If you don't know where you are going, you will wind up somewhere else.
- You can observe a lot just by watching.
- He must have made that before he died. (Referring to a Steve McQueen movie)
- Slump? I ain't in no slump. I just ain't hitting.
- A nickel isn't worth a dime today.
- I take a two hour nap, from one o'clock to four.
- If I didn't wake up, I'd still be sleeping.
- Why buy good luggage? You only use it when you travel.
- I knew I was going to take the wrong train, so I left early

Those two gentlemen alone have added immeasurably to the humorous side of language, but it doesn't end there. Irish Bulls occur in news interviews, in overheard conversations, in political speeches, on TV talk shows, and in countless other venues. They are *udderly* delightful; I hope they never stop.

- Half the lies my opponents tell about me are not true.
- This newspaper article is full of omissions.
- I marvel at the strength of human weakness.
- The food here is terrible, and the portions are too small.

- I was permanently disabled for almost a year.
- Computers are not intelligent. They only think they are.
- Always be sincere, even when you don't mean it.
- We must believe in free will. We have no choice.
- She wouldn't recognize subtlety if it hit her like a ton of bricks.
- Like everybody else, I'll be first in line to buy a ticket.
- Nostalgia ain't what it used to be.
- It's not a hallucination; it just feels like one.
- Anarchy may not be the best form of government, but it's better than no government at all.
- At first, I had second thoughts.
- If we stop to look at everything, we won't have time to see anything.
- Every minute was more exciting than the next.
- The simpler things become, the more complicated they are.
- He gets up at six o'clock no matter what time it is.
- I always like the same thing: variety.
- It takes a lot of preparation to be spontaneous.
- Just because they're identical twins, it doesn't mean they're alike.
- Can't it wait till yesterday?
- I believe we are on an irreversible trend...but that could change.
- I distinctly remember forgetting that.
- I have opinions of my own—strong opinions—but I don't always agree with them.
- As far as I know, my computer has never had an undetected error.
- It's very important to pay attention to trivial matters.
- I remember my house full of people, but I don't remember anybody being there.
- I used to think I was indecisive, but now I'm not so sure.
- I'm going to live through this if it kills me!
- I'm sorry, but I'm not going to apologize.
- I have nine different drawings, but some of them are the same.
- Within three weeks, you should see instant improvement.
- Never listen to advice.
- There is a time for talking and a time for remaining silent. This is not one of them.

- Predestination was doomed from the start.
- I'm so sick, I almost feel good.
- Secret conversations are not allowed.
- Most of the time, you have to be on guard all of the time.
- He sideswiped the front of my truck.
- At the airport, avoid transporting items without your knowledge.
- She's afraid they'll starve to death for the rest of their lives.
- It's the same difference.
- The generating of random numbers is far too important to be left to chance.
- There's no future in time travel.
- Their styles are unique in many similar ways.
- I practically had to hit them over the head to convince them that I'm a pacifist.
- You should have been there after you left.
- Nothing is more than the most.
- What sane person could live in this world and not be crazy?
- Describe what an invisible airplane would look like.
- Spare no expense to make everything as economical as possible.
- The only way to keep things the same is to change.
- I'm not the same person I always wanted to be.
- Fertility is hereditary. If your parents didn't have any children, neither will you.

WORD HISTORIES

One of the delights of language is studying how words begin and develop. Sometimes there is such a variance in what a word originally meant and what it means now that we are startled. Occasionally, the origin sheds historical light on why our current meaning came to be, but quite often it simply highlights the quirkiness of vocabulary development.

Let's do a quick alphabetical review on a handful of such words.

agony

We're talking about industrial-strength suffering here, both mental and physical. Thanks to what has been memorialized in all four Gospel accounts, most people associate this word with Christ's Agony in the Garden. Agony doesn't get more intense than that.

The word started out in Greek as the verb *to act* (agein), and in some contexts it eventually meant *to torture*. As a noun, it referred to contests in ancient Greece, involving either athletic or musical competitions, in which prizes were awarded to the winners. To agonize in those days was to go all-out in competition. Just do it.

As time went on, it was used to describe a conflict between characters in drama and in literature. The word entered English with the sense of mental suffering, then was extended to physical suffering. Paradoxically, it has also been used in a positive sense, as when Alexander Pope spoke of "cries and agonies of wild delight" [Odyssey x. 492].

bankrupt

As a noun, this signifies a person or corporation considered legally insolvent; as a verb, it means to ruin, whether financially or morally.

There is some confusion here, but it seems that it comes from the Italian *banca rotta*, which some interpret as *broken bench*. According to this story, when a trader failed to pay his creditors, his place of business was closed up by the authorities, and his bench (counter) was smashed into pieces. Those with a less colorful interpretation say that *rotta* simply meant interrupted or stopped, and that no sledgehammers were involved. I prefer the sound and the fury.

cartoon

We consider cartoons to be a form of entertainment, something humorous but ephemeral. In times gone by, cartoons served a far more more serious purpose.

We find the seminal word *carta* in Latin, where it meant paper. As it was assimilated into Italian and French, it came to mean strong, heavy paper, a type of pasteboard. Rather than being covered with frivolous, inconsequential drawings, such pasteboard was used by serious artists to plot preliminary drawings of what were to become international masterpieces. Think of Da Vinci's notebooks.

If you've ever moved from one place to another without hiring a moving company, you've scurried around looking for a cartoon's close relative: cardboard cartons to be filled with your earthly possessions.

debauch

We debauch people when we corrupt their morals or principles. We lead them astray from their duties or proper allegiances. Often, impurity or unchaste actions are involved. Ethical erosion is at the heart of the matter.

That's why it's interesting to learn that the word arose from carpenters and masons chipping away at building materials. The carpenter would rough-hew a timber, as opposed to building fine furniture with perfectly smooth surfaces. In other words, he would hack away at the timber just enough to produce a relatively flat surface; you could still see the hack marks when he was finished. Such timbers often acted as roof supports, and to this day, that rough hewn aspect is a prized feature.

In the case of the stonemason, he would hack away at a row or course of stones in order to make them serviceably flat. At one point in history, a *bauche* was a hut built of stones. So, just as a builder would change materials from their original, pristine state, so would the debaucher hack away at the soul of the innocent.

easel

An easel has become the unmistakable symbol of an artist. It is the upright frame, usually tripodal, upon which the blank canvas is placed, and which can even be used to display the finished product. It is functional, inert, and unmoving.

So it is startling to learn that the word originally meant an ass—not the insulting kind or the fat-laden kind, but the beast of burden. The Dutch word *ezel* referred to a donkey, and a donkey was a working animal that carried things.

So loading a braying animal with goods to be transported morphed into a device used to hold beautiful paintings.

fulcrum

A fulcrum is defined as the point or support on which a lever pivots. I always associate it with physics, probably because of Archimedes' famous boast: "Give me a place to stand and with a lever I will move the whole world." That place to stand would have been his fulcrum.

However, according to the origin of the word, Archimedes could have saved his energy and stayed in bed. The Latin verb *fulcire* meant to support or prop up, which fits in nicely with the fulcrum/lever image. But when the noun *fulcrum* developed from that verb, it had a quite specific meaning. It meant a bed post. There were usually four of them, and their function was to raise the bed from the drafty floor.

garble

Speech can be garbled—distorted, scrambled, difficult to understand—if you use a cheap cell phone. And facts can be garbled if data are twisted or used in a misleading way. Comprehensive research and a grasp of reality are our best friends.

But the word started out in a much more mundane way. Following connections through Anglo-Norman (*garbeler*), Arabic (*girbal*), and Latin (*cribrum*), we discover that the connecting idea is a sieve—that meshed or perforated device used for sifting, straining, and purifying. In the old days, when you garbled something—especially precious spices—you were removing debris and impurities, making the spices enticing to use and to sell. By the 17th century, it had come to mean confused or distorted speech or ideas.

haggard

After a long night of hard work (or intense dissipation), we can't be blamed for looking worn, exhausted, and gaunt. Haggard is inevitable under those conditions.

But long ago, the base of the word was used only in referring to wild falcons. The *hag* portion meant woods, copse, or hedge, and that's where an untamed, wild falcon would be found.

As time went by, the word was transferred to the wild-eyed look that a human might have, then developed the meaning of careworn.

idiot

I know that I have felt like an idiot countless times in my life, but we're sometimes too harsh on ourselves—or on others. Once upon a time, this word was used as a technical classification of mental abilities, but that type of classification is now understood to be inaccurate and offensive. We use idiot as an epithet for someone we consider stupid or reckless.

In ancient Greek, the word had a range of meanings. At its core, it meant a private person, but that had more negative connotations than we would expect today. A private person selfishly catered to his own affairs; he did not engage in public service. A private person had no professional knowledge; she was a layperson in the limited sense of that word. And a form of the word idiot was also applied to foot soldiers—the cannon fodder (in later centuries) of the military world.

jeopardy

Aside from being the thinking person's favorite game show, today jeopardy is a relentlessly one-sided word. It screams danger and peril, the possibility of losing life, property, reputation, freedom, or anything else that we prize.

But when the word started, it was less one-sided; it was more balanced and equitable. In Old French, it was *jeu parti,* and it meant a divided game, divided in the sense of even chances for both sides. It involved a game that depended upon strategy, such as chess, a game that could go either way. The *jeu* segment derived from the Latin *jocus,* a jest or a joke.

By the 14th century, jeopardy had picked up the univocal sense of risk and danger.

knapsack

This word figures prominently in the song *Happy Wanderer,* a German import sung by generations of American Scouts: "I love to go a-wandering/Along the mountain track/And as I go, I love to sing/My knapsack on my back."

The *-sack* half of the word is obvious. We tend to use the word backpack, but it's the same convenient carrier.

The history of the *knap-* portion is a bit obscure, but it seems to come from German and/or Dutch words meaning to eat. That word in turn came from an earlier word meaning to chip a stone with sharp blows. The implication, therefore, is that it's the kind of eating where you bite off small pieces of something, rather than sitting down to a sumptious dinner.

So the knapsack was a snack sack—food on the run.

lunatic

While lunatic is used to designate a crazy or very foolish person, these days we use a much softened sense of this word. "He's a lunatic" can be said with admiration; think Bill Murray.

A few centuries back, lunatic and insane were a technical pair. Insanity was a permanent condition, chronic in nature. Lunacy was intermittent; there were periods of lucidity.

But what triggered the bouts of lunacy? The ancient Romans thought they knew: it was the phases of the moon. A waxing moon brought lucidity; a full moon brought out the wolf man in us. And the Roman word for moon? It was *luna,* of course.

muscle

A muscle man may drive a muscle car and try to muscle in where he's not appreciated, but even he can't escape the age-old question: are you a man or a mouse?

In Latin, *musculum* meant a little mouse. The conceit was that the rippling of muscles under the skin (think biceps, for instance) looked very much like the motion of mice under a piece of cloth or sacking.

The Greeks had the same idea. For them, the word *mys* had two equally apt meanings: field mouse and muscle. From that source we derived the much-used medical combining form *myo-* (muscle): myoatrophy, myocardial, myocele, and hundreds more.

nausea

We all know that it's easy to be queasy, especially on roller coasters and airplanes. This word took root in an ancient form of travel.

In Greek, a *nautes* was a sailor, and he shipped out on a *naus*. So the original nausea was seasickness, though it has expanded to many potential causes and is even used to signify emotional or ethical loathing.

By the way, its inelegant cousin, puke, seems to be onomatopoetic: it imitates the sound made by a person throwing up. Oddly enough, Shakespeare may have been the first writer to use the word. In Jacques' Seven Ages of Man speech (*As You Like It*), we find, "At first the infant, mewling and puking in the nurse's arms."

orient

Orienteering is a sport or pursuit growing in popularity. The purists use compasses and folding maps. Their wealthier counterparts carry elaborate and expensive GPS devices. In all cases, getting your directions straight is the goal.

The older amongst us will remember Lamont Cranston, "who, while in the Orient, learned the power to cloud men's minds." Even if you don't remember *The Shadow*, you know that the Orient stands for the Asian nations.

It started before compasses. One of the simplest directions to discern for the Romans was *oriens*, that point on the horizon at which the sun rises each morning. In the European Christian era, since Jesus' homeland was to the east, it was a requirement that altars be oriented—facing east, that is.

pilgrim

Here's a word that was used by John Wayne in several of his westerns, usually addressing a stranger on his way through town. That was entirely appropriate.

The word started life in Latin as two words: *per* (through) and *ager* (field). This led to the word *pereger*, someone traveling abroad. That, in turn led to peregrinus, a foreigner. Over the course of centuries, this was transmuted in English to a form of pilgrim.

We have retained the fancy word peregrination to denote a journey, and we know that there is a peregrine falcon.

See **xenophobia**

queue

Here's a word with several seemingly diverse meanings: an orderly line of people; a sequence of stored computer data awaiting processing; a pigtail hanging down one's back.

The word entered English from the French, which in turn had borrowed it from Latin. The original source was *cauda,* the tail of an animal.

So those various meanings have a thread running through them. Picture a tail hanging down and you're not far from the line of people, the waiting data, and the plait of hair. And in music, the concluding or closing part of a movement or composition is called a coda. Same animal.

rumination

This is a five-dollar word for thought, ponderous ideas, meditation. We certainly don't associate these higher intellectual processes with a cow standing in a field, but there is an inescapable connection.

It goes back in a straight line to the Latin word *ruminari,* to chew the cud. This is something that cows, members of the ruminant classification, do interminably. Ruminants—which also include sheep, goats, bison, llamas, antelope, deer, and giraffes—are hooved animals that characteristically have stomachs divided into four compartments. The first compartment is the rumen, and cud is regurgitated, partially digested food. The food moves through all four chambers eventually, but the process of digestion takes place in stages.

sunbeam

A warm, comfort-filled word, but quirky nonetheless. It is, of course, a ray of sunshine, so the *sun-* segment makes perfect sense, but what about a beam? I associate that with the huge piece of timber used in construction to hold up the roof.

As it turns out, so did the scholar who invented the word. We're talking about Alfred the Great, who translated several key works from Latin to Old English. While he was translating Bede's *Ecclesiastical History of the English People* (translation of the Latin title), he kept bumping up against the image *columna lucis*, which we would now translate as "column of light." King Alfred didn't have the word column in his contemporary vocabulary, so he reached for the nearest reality: bêam, a tree or building post. So a sunbeam was a sun post was a *columna lucis*.

trophy

Somewhere in your house, probably on a tabletop or mantel, you have a cup, plaque, or statuette won by your child in a sporting contest, a spelling bee, or some other endeavor. Or you may have a trophy wife or husband. At any rate, the word is familiar and in popular use.

The original trophy, the Greek *tropaios*, was not something you'd want in your home. A trophy in those days was a monument of sorts erected on a battlefield to commemorate a rout—a crushing, bloody defeat of the enemy. *Tropaios* signified a turning, a decisive movement, and arms and equipment salvaged from the dead and mutilated bodies of the enemy would be hung from a tree branch or piled up on a beach.

The Romans preferred to erect architectural memorials such as arches and massive monuments. We've downsized the whole affair to little statues that even a child can lift in personal triumph.

umbrage

The polite lady or gentleman takes umbrage. The vulgar and loutish person gets pissed off. Umbrage, therefore, is resentment or offense.

The source of this refined word is the Latin word *umbra*, shadow or darkness. When you take umbrage, it's as if a shadow has fallen over your existence; sunbeams fail to reach you. You have been plunged into darkness. Doom and gloom ensue.

Another word that comes from this root is umbrella. We associate it with rain, but fair-skinned patrician women used the device to preserve the complexion. You know you're a redneck if…

vaccine

Medically, we live in a marvelous era. The proliferation

of vaccines to protect us against vicious diseases proceeds with comforting speed. Some previously universal killers have been all but eradicated. So where did this comforting word come from?

Ruminate on this: the Latin word for cow was *vacca*. We may thank Edward Jenner for the word vaccine and for the success of a vaccine against smallpox. Smallpox was a killer in the 18th century, and the procedure in vogue when Jenner became a physician was to deliberately infect people with a small dose of smallpox. The problem was twofold: the person inoculated could just as easily die as receive immunity, and he or she was now a carrier of the dreaded disease.

Jenner was aware of the farm worker's belief that people who had suffered a non-lethal case of cowpox would not contract smallpox. He did rigorous research on this belief and finally proved scientifically that it was true.

waffle

Let's focus not on the breakfast item (from a Dutch word that alluded to a honeycomb or woven item), but on the political or public office sense. When a politician or CEO waffles, he or she is vacillating, equivocating, blowing smoke in order to conceal.

It's almost as annoying as the yapping of a pint-sized dog, and that's where the word seems to have originated in 17th century England. "Waff/waff" was someone's imitation of an ear swab getting up in your face. Larger dogs with bigger chest cavities were thought to say "woof/woof."

xenophobia

John Wayne may have encountered quite a few pilgrims, but he didn't seem to be afraid of them. Come to think of it, though, his best advice was to sit with your back to a wall when visiting a rowdy saloon.

If he had been afraid of strangers, he would have been termed a xenophobe (pronounced zenophobe). This is because the Greek word part *xeno-* comes from a word that means stranger or foreigner. *Phob-* indicates strong aversion or even fear.

The word part *xeno-* is particularly useful in medicine, where we encounter terms such as *xenobiotic* (foreign to the body or to living organisms) or *xenograft* (in which the donor and the recipient come from different species)

yen

Not the monetary unit, but the strong desire or yearning or craving or inclination: *She has a yen for the strong, silent type.*

We all have yens, but the word actually started as a word meaning an addiction to narcotics—specifically, opium. Nineteenth-century Chinese immigrants brought with them the word *yan*, meaning a craving for opium. There were variant spellings depending on the dialect. We find this in H. A. Giles' 1876 *Chinese Sketches*: "Chinamen ask if an opium-smoker has the *yin* or not; meaning thereby, has he gradually increased his doses of opium until he has established a craving for the drug."

So while we toss the word around to signify a craving for chocolate or for a Big Mac, it once had a heavy-duty and terrible denotation.

zero

Expressed by the numeral 0, it means absence of measurement or of value: zip, nada, nothing.

It was heavily influenced by the Italian word *zefiro* (shortened to zero in English), a word borrowed from the Arabic *sifr*, which meant empty. That Arabic word also supplied us with cipher, which, at one point in history, was a doublet for zero. In more recent history, we have tended to treat the word cipher as a synonym for a secret code.

SURVIVING
LANGUAGE ONLINE

While the internet is a gold mine of information, it also contains an unbelievable amount of misinformation. Unfortunately, much of the garbage involves language—word and phrase origins in particular.

Every one of the language myths explored in Chapter 10 may be found online. In fact, you don't even have to go online to encounter them; someone is bound to send you an email telling you definitively where this word or that phrase or some other grammar requirement came from. Nine times out of ten, they will contain folk etymology—language myths too easily and unthinkingly perpetuated by hitting the forward button.

You should especially be wary of bulletin boards that encourage readers to send in their theories and speculations, bouncing wild guesses back and forth. Since language fine-tuning is so complicated—it requires knowledge of advanced research techniques, history, morphology, etymology, psychology, and a host of other skills—it is no place to honor false democracy; my opinion is as good as the next person's is simply not true when it comes to complicated fields such as language. In those BB venues, inventiveness is preferred over plodding research, and a good story is often prized over accuracy.

But instead of railing about well-intentioned amateurs or reviewing once again the tedious requirements for accurate linguistic analysis, I'm going to give you a checklist of some web sites that can be trusted. I'll break them down into categories, since you won't be looking for reliable information on the same topic or subset each time. My only hope is that they will still be in business down the road when you need them. The web is notorious for fast turnovers.

UNABRIDGED DICTIONARIES

American Heritage Dictionary
• www.bartleby.com/am/

This is the 4th edition, produced in the year 2000. Not only will you find 90,000 entries, but at least 75% of the words provide you with audio pronunciations. A simple search box allows you a choice: entry word, full text, definition, etymology, entries with notes, and articles.

The Contents section allows you to browse through Bibliographic Record, Entry Index, Illustrations, Pronunciation Key, Articles Index, and Charts and Tables.

Entries with Notes includes these choices: Regional Notes, Our Living Language Notes, Synonym Notes, Usage Notes, and Word History Notes. AHD is justly famous for presenting Indo-European roots (also published as a separate booklet), and they will be found in an appendix. Other appendices explain what Indo-European is, and Semitic roots are presented in an appendix, as well as their history.

Webster's Unabridged (1913)
• www.machaut.uchicago.edu/?resource=Webster%27s (search features)
• www.bibliomania.com/2/3/257/frameset.html

This warning is clearly displayed on the U of C version: "Remember, these are 1913 and 1828 editions and will not contain some modern words." But it's hard to beat this dictionary for words that endured until the early 20th century. Academic or specialized terms of historical interest that might be found in few other places will be found here.

The search box at the University of Chicago site offers several choices:

• You may enter a single word and press search. Only that word is returned.

• You may enter a word or word portion, check off Float, and find all the words containing those letters. For instance, entering the word power in the float mode will return power, powerful, overpowering, etc.

• You may use the wild card symbol. For instance, entering "r*pe" will return rape, ripe, and rope. For some reason, wild card searches are better on an older version: www.humanities.uchicago.edu/orgs/ARTFL/forms_unrest/webster.form.html

• You may choose between two editions, 1828 and 1913. The historical benefits are obvious.

This site also contains the 1911 edition of Roget's Thesaurus, French-English and English-French Dictionaries, and a French Conjugator which will lead you through the intricacies of French verbs.

Century Dictionary
• www.global-language.com/century

To make this site work, you need to download the free DjVu image compression software with a simple click of a button. The software—somewhat more sophisticated than .pdf format, according to its authors—allows you to control what you see onscreen. In fact, you may choose from simple DjVu, DjVu highlighted, Java, or JPEG.

This dictionary, no longer published after the 1914 edition, is still one of the largest English language dictionaries in existence, and many scholars consider it the finest American dictionary ever produced. Words entering English after 1914 will not be available, of course, but your collegiate dictionary will cover those.

The search box allows you to seek individual words or entire phrases, and it accepts Boolean searches that will bring more precise returns. (If you're not familiar with Boolean logic and commands, you'll find clear information at http://library.albany.edu/internet/boolean.html). You may also simply browse entries alphabetically. With all its superb features, I'm amazed that this online version is free.

Oxford English Dictionary
   • www.oed.com

This is the granddaddy of modern English dictionaries, but it doesn't come free. Individual subscribers are charged $29.95 per month or $295 per year. If your work requires you to use words precisely, you should consider subscribing. You might check to see if your local public or academic library subscribes as an institution and allows public access.

OED does offer a free Word of the Day by email. To register for this service, visit   http://www.oed.com/services/email-wotd.html

GENERAL DICTIONARIES

Cambridge Dictionary
   • www.dictionary.cambridge.org/

You have a choice of several dictionaries here, so you might want to select the Cambridge Dictionary of American English from the menu if that's where you live. This gives ungarnished returns, but the search box is simple to use.

Selections include these dictionaries: Advanced Learner's, Learner's, Idioms, Phrasal Verbs, French/English, and Spanish/English.
There is a Word-a-Day feature, but it doesn't come via email. You'll find it at www.dictionary.cambridge.org/wordoftheday.asp

Dictionary.com
   • www.Dictionary.com
This site is popular because it is a multi-source dictionary. That is, more than one dictionary is consulted when you perform a search. Its data bank includes
The American Heritage Dictionary of the English Language (Fourth Edition),

Webster's Revised Unabridged Dictionary (1913),
WordNet 1.6, 1997 Princeton University,
The Free On-line Dictionary of Computing, Jargon File 4.2.0,
CIA World Factbook (1995),
Easton's 1897 Bible Dictionary,
Hitchcock's Bible Names Dictionary,
U.S. Gazetteer,
U.S. Census Bureau.

The dates warn us that very recent terms may not be included.

The site contains many other language resources, and there is a premium subscription service with full features. There is also a free Word-a-Day email service. Sign up at www.signup.dictionary.com/wordoftheday

OneLook Dictionaries
  • www.onelook.com/

This is a very useful site. Notice that the search box must be checked to indicate "Find definitions," "Find translations," or "Search all dictionaries." (They claim to search well over 900 online dictionaries.) Wild card searches allow two branches: use ? to indicate one missing letter, and * to indicate any number of missing letters. They give examples to help you.

Particularly useful is the reverse dictionary that lets you describe a concept to get a word:
  www.onelook.com/reverse-dictionary.shtml

And unlike most other similar sites, this one allows extensive customization. Their Word-a-Day feature gives five words instead of one, and they are pegged to web inquiries:
  www.onelook.com/?c=wotd

Merriam-Webster Online
  • www.m-w.com/info/pr/addenda.htm

This is a good old workhorse, but if you want more than brief entries, you'll have to subscribe to Merriam-Webster Collegiate or Merriam-Webster Unabridged. Access to that information will be found at the top of the page. The online version has only a simple word entry box, but the returns include an audio file that says the word out loud.

AWAD (A Word A Day)
  • www.wordsmith.org/awad/

This is not a dictionary per se, but since 1994, webmeister Anu Garg has amassed a hefty list of words. You may access an alphabetical list at
  • wordsmith.org/awad/wordlist.html

The weekly offerings are arranged by theme. Access that list at wordsmith.org/awad/themes.html

AWAD also ships one of the most famous Word-a-Day lists via email: see
  www.wordsmith.org/awad/faq.html#sub

THESAURI

The word thesaurus comes from a Latin word meaning treasury. Besides its meaning as a treasury or storehouse, it more commonly means a listing of words with similar or related meanings. Some versions will also list antonyms.

Roget's II, New Thesaurus, 3rd Edition
  • www.bartleby.com/62/

Webster's Thesaurus
  • www.m-w.com/thesaurus.htm

Your Dictionary Thesaurus
  • www.yourdictionary.com/

SPECIALIZED DICTIONARIES

The following entries do not need detailed descriptions; each title will tell you whether the site will be useful in your current search. If any of the URLs are broken by the time you get around to them, insert the title in a google search box and fire away.

Brewer's Dictionary of Phrase and Fable
  • www.bartleby.com/81/

Business/Finance Dictionary
- www.nytimes.com/library/financial/glossary/bfglosa.htm

Computing Dictionary
- wombat.doc.ic.ac.uk/foldoc/

Construction Dictionary
- www.glossarist.com/glossaries/business/construction.asp

Crossword Puzzle Dictionary
- www.oneacross.com/

Etymology Dictionary
- www.etymonline.com/

Food Dictionary
- www.epicurious.com/cooking/how_to/food_dictionary/

Foreign Language Dictionaries
- www.dir.yahoo.com/Reference/Dictionaries/Language/

Geological Terms Dictionary
- www.a-z-dictionaries.com/Geological_terms_dictionary.html

Legal Dictionary
- www.dictionary.law.com/default2.asp?typed=

Life Sciences Dictionary
- www.biotech.icmb.utexas.edu/search/dict-search.html

Literary Dictionary
- www.galegroup.com/free_resources/glossary/

Management Jargon Dictionary
- www.geocities.com/Athens/Styx/8877/mj/mj.html

Medical Dictionary
- www.intelihealth.com/IH/ihtIHWSIHW000/9276/9276.html

Mortgage Dictionary
- www.glossarist.com/glossaries/economy-finance/mortgage.asp

Multiple Specialty Dictionaries
- www.yourdictionary.com/diction5a.html
- www.yourdictionary.com/diction4.html
- www.angli02.kgw.tu-berlin.de/call/webofdic/diction4.html
- www.linguistlist.org/sp/Dict.html

Music Dictionary
- www.library.thinkquest.org/2791/MDOPNSCR.htm
- www.schirmerdictionary-d.wadsworth.com/

Philosophy Dictionary
- www.philosophypages.com/dy/

Rap Dictionary
- www.rapdict.org/wiki/index.php/Category:Terms

Rhyming Dictionary
- www.rhymezone.com/

Science Dictionary
- www.glossarist.com/glossaries/science/

Sign Language Dictionary
- www.commtechlab.msu.edu/sites/aslweb/browser.htm
- www..masterstech-home.com/ASLDict.html

Slang Dictionary
- www.OCF.Berkeley.EDU/~wrader/slang/

Sports Dictionary
- www.glossarist.com/glossaries/sports-recreation/

Theological Dictionary
- www.a-z-dictionaries.com/theological_dictionary.html

TRUSTWORTHY WORD & PHRASE SITES

Take Our Word For It
- www.takeourword.com/

This site used to issue a weekly email. Recently, distribution has been spotty. However, issues 1 through 197 are archived under

the title "Back Issues." You'll find an internal search engine at
http://www.takeourword.com/search.html

The Word Detective
• www.word-detective.com/
The Word Detective is written by Evan Morris and appears
in newspapers in the U.S., Mexico, and Japan. Hundreds of words
and phrases indexed in alphabetical order are contained in his web
archive. Click "Archives" or jump directly to www.word-detective.
com/backidx.html

Word Origins
• www.wordorigins.org/
Scroll down to "The Big List" for a large archive. The webmeister
also distributes a free weekly electronic newsletter on words and
themes. On the page above, subscription information will be found
in the third block of information.
There is also a discussion group, but I would be careful. While
the moderator will jump in with corrections on occasion, you'll find
some mistaken notions posted by contributors. Sometimes they
are enshrined in the BB archive. The good news is that the site is
currently undergoing an extensive update.

Word Spy
• www.wordspy.com/
Webmaster Paul McFedries introduces his site this way: "This
Web site is devoted to lexpionage, the sleuthing of new words and
phrases. These aren't 'stunt words' or 'sniglets,' but new terms that
have appeared multiple times in newspapers, magazines, books,
Web sites, and other recorded sources."
So this is a specialty site that covers relatively recent coinages.
Alphabetical archives may be found toward the bottom of the
page.

World Wide Words
• www.worldwidewords.org/
Sections on this word site by Michael Quinion include Articles,
Questions & Answers, Reviews, Topical Words, Turns of Phrase,
and Weird Words. The moderator provides citations and advice for
the Oxford English Dictionary, so his work is well researched.

The site offers an interesting free weekly newsletter distributed electronically. Click on "Join the World Wide Words mailing list" to subscribe.

You would do well, when you encounter a word site not listed here, to cross check what it contains with the sites listed above. A sure kiss of death is finding one of the mistakes listed in Chapter 10 presented as the truth.

SQUINTING, STRAGGLING, & DANGLING

One devilish feature of our language is straying modifiers. There are many adjectives and adverbs that click neatly and logically into place, but the ones that slip and slide can lead to confusing or unintentionally funny messages.

The squinting modifier is a case at hand. It is a modifier that is placed in a pivotal position; it might describe or limit the word to its left or the word to its right.

Employees who come to work late frequently get fired.

Does this mean that they frequently are late or that they are frequently fired? Common sense will solve that one, but the question never should have arisen in the first place.

The firemen who fled the burning room quickly recovered from smoke inhalation.

Did they flee quickly or did they recover quickly? Not placing the modifier in the exact spot leads to confusion.

A variation on the squinting modifier is the doubly applicable modifier. It's easier if we start with some examples.

A baby doctor: is this an infant who practices medicine, or a pediatrician?

A paper clip: is this a clip made of paper, or a clip designed to hold paper?

A bald tire inspector: who's bald—the inspector or the tire?

A hand chopper: does this remove hands, or is it held in the hand?

The source of the ambiguity is that the opening word could be applied in a couple of directions. The writer's intention is paramount, but there is room for the reader's (mis)interpretation.

- criminal law professor: a law professor who has turned to crime?
- small business owner: the very short woman who owns the clothing store?
- big city dweller: 300 pound tenant?
- tall ship captain: bumps his head on the mast?
- plastic hair clips: to restrain plastic hair?
- bad golf ball: designed to prevent you from playing good golf?
- huge author list: no writer under 250 pounds?
- new car salesman: hired only yesterday?
- vicious dog owner: his bite is worse than his bark?
- dangerous sport specialist: don't turn your back on him?
- dirty book salesman: she needs a shower?
- polluted well inspector: check for hidden liquor bottles?
- bankrupt business analyst: don't take her financial advice?
- bald tire inspector: get that man a toupee?
- small apartment owner: appeared in the Wizard of Oz?
- noxious weed inspector: pull him up by the roots?
- tough love counselor: don't get into an argument with her?
- bad attitude adjustment: try adjusting again?
- strange phenomena expert: and have you met his wife?
- antique car dealer: was he a pal of Henry Ford?
- small arms dealer: too short to see over the counter?
- easy chair upholsterer: nothing difficult about him at all?
- sick house expert: give him two aspirins?
- weak force theorist: feed him vitamins?
- crazy glue salesman: don't get on his bad side?
- oriental rug salesman: is he always Wong?

It all leads to a conundrum: if salted peanuts are peanuts that have salt on them, then why aren't shelled walnuts walnuts that still have their shells on?

Oddly enough, this wasn't that much of a problem when English was in its infancy. In its Old English form, spelling indicated connection. You could place an adjective anywhere in the sentence without divorcing it from its partner. This was called a synthetic system, and we can use a Latin example to drive the point home.

Canis parva dominum magnum habet = the small dog has a large owner.

A quick primer: because of its spelling, canis (dog) is the subject of the sentence. Again because of its spelling, parva (small) can apply only to the dog. Dominum (owner) has to be the object of the verb; spelling dictates that. Magnum (large) can apply only to dominum [notice the shared ending –um].

So here's the crucial point: in a synthetic language, even if you move the words around, the meaning never changes—all of the following arrangements mean precisely the same thing: the small dog has a large owner.

Parva habet magnum dominum canis.
Dominum canis magnum parva habet.
Habet canis dominum magnum parva.   etc.

But modern English is a totally different animal. It is now an analytic language: we figure out meaning by position. Words cannot be scrambled without losing the original meaning. Quick proof:

The small dog has a large owner.
The large dog has a small owner.
Owner dog large small the a has.

So when we write, yet one more obligation is placing adjectives and adverbs—whether single words or phrases—precisely where they will make the most sense.

Among the funniest errors perpetrated by poor placement are dangling modifiers. Sometimes the error consists in not supplying a clear subject.

Slamming on the brakes, the car skidded into a tree.

    (The car slammed on the brakes?)

When I slammed on the brakes, the car skidded into a tree.

    (Subject now supplied.)

Sometimes the simple solution to correcting the dangling modifier is moving it closer to the word it actually modifies.

    I found my missing wallet cleaning my room.

    (The wallet was cleaning your room?)

    While I was cleaning my room, I found my missing wallet.

So let's stroll down ludicrous lane and see what happens when we place modifiers carelessly.

- Oozing slowly across the table, Marvin watched the spilled salad dressing.
- Pressing the button, the elevator went down to the basement.
- With his tail held high, my father led his prize poodle around the ring.
- I saw the dead dog driving down Interstate 75.
- By the age of ten, both of Patricia's parents had died.
- Hidden behind the billboard, the motorists could not see the policeman.
- She handed out brownies to the children stored in ZipLoc bags.
- After sitting all night in the marinade, I put the roast in the oven.
- A woman hurried by, leading a Neapolitan Mastiff in a long black dress.
- Covered in strawberry jam, my friends will love these homemade muffins.
- After eating all their food, we put the cats outside.
- At the beginning of the novel, Tom Joad comes across a turtle on his way home from spending four years in prison.
- Hopping eratically through the flower garden, I saw a frog.
- My cousin went on interminably, describing the details of her wedding in the elevator.
- Captain Ahab relentlessly pursued the while whale with a wooden leg.
- Don't try to pet the dog on the porch that is growling.
- I bought the Venus statue from the new shop owner with the

missing arms.
- The smoke alarm went off while cooking my dinner.
- Looking out the airplane window, the volcano seemed ready to erupt.
- We saw several giraffes on vacation in Africa.
- Reading a book, my cat crawled into my lap.
- We saw a herd of sheep on the way to our hotel in Wales.
- Dipped in chocolate, many people love fresh strawberries.
- A tarantula bit one of the banana packers that had a hairy, huge body.
- I glimpsed a rat sorting the recyclable cardboard.
- I sent a poster to Mom rolled in a tube.
- Sitting on the telephone wire, he saw a robin.
- While doing the dishes, a cockroach ran across the floor.

ABOUT THE AUTHOR

Michael Sheehan was born in Chicago and raised on its notorious South Side, an area documented by novels such as Studs Lonigan, The Jungle, The Man with the Golden Arm, and many others. At age 16, he escaped a life of certain crime by entering a seminary in Saugatuck, Michigan, and after that, his studies took him all over the Midwest: Oconomowoc, Wisconsin, Conception and St. Louis, Missouri, and back to Olympia Fields, Illinois. He received a B.A. in philosophy from Villanova University, an M.A. in English from DePaul University, and did postgraduate studies at the University of Chicago. Eventually, he taught English classes for 26 years at Olive-Harvey College, (located on the southeast side of Chicago) a branch of the City Colleges of Chicago. He is a member of the Society of Midland Authors, the Dictionary Society of North America, and Michigan Writers. He gives seminars and presentations on language all over the state of Michigan.

On the Lamb in a Doggy-Dog World: At Play With the English Language, is a follow-up to *Words to the Wise: A Lighthearted Look at the English Language*. Words to the Wise was based on transcripts from Sheehan's weekly radio show on WTCM, Talk Radio 580, originating in Traverse City, Michigan. A call-in show, it airs each Tuesday morning from 9:00 to 10:00.

Sheehan has written seven other books:

Words to the Wise: A Lighthearted Look at the English Language
(Arbutus Press, 2004)
The Word Parts Dictionary (McFarland & Co., 2000)
Words! A Vocabulary Power Workbook (Harcourt Brace, 1996)
Handbook for Basic Writers (Prentice-Hall, 1991)
Workbook for Basic Writers (Prentice-Hall, 1991)
The Cry of the Jackal (Avalon Books, 1991)
In the Shadow of the Bear (Avalon Books, 1990)